THE LJ WAY

THE ROADMAP TO YOUR JOURNEY FROM POVERTY TO PLENTY

The LJ Way
The Roadmap To Your Journey From Poverty to Plenty
By LaSonjia Jack

Copyright 2024
All Rights Reserved
ISBN # 979-8-218-32336-3

Published By PrintRaven

Dedication

This book is dedicated to my two sons, Myles David Jack and Jahlen Bryce Jack. The stories told in this book have been shared with them along the way, as I sought to find my inner greatness.

Before you two were born, I dreamed of having children and spoke to each of you individually while I was pregnant, promising to do something great. I prayed for you both, equally. I dreamed of being a "Boy Mom" and all the adventures we would have together. I have tried to be your true role model in all that I have accomplished and what I have yet to do. I wake up each morning smiling because of the men you both are and what GOD has in store for you in the future. My decision to write this book is based on my passion to help others succeed and find their way in the world. You two are beautiful children of GOD that I carry on my back each day.

I am so proud to be your mother, business partner, confidant, and an overall POSITIVE support system that will never leave your side. Our family motto is "WE Always DO our BEST, no Matter What." I love you both more than anything else in the world, and I will continue to show you both in various ways. The accolades I have achieved in the business world some would call success, but my life being both of your mother is what I call phenomenal. That has always been my focus and driving force. Love you both and can't wait to see what you will create for the generations beyond us.

Acknowledgements

First, I would like to thank GOD for making me the person who shines her light on others.
2 Chronicles 15:7 (NIV) ~ But as for you, be strong and do not give up, for your work will be rewarded.

To my beautiful mother, Pastor Minyon A. Perrin: The woman who brought me into the world and never stops supporting her family. Your daily prayers and commitment to God have protected this family, and those prayers continue to bring us blessings upon blessings. Thank you for allowing me to "shine" in my own unique way.

To my heavenly dad, Carlos Van Fisher: I have received so many of your characteristics, from the love of music, how to maneuver in the workforce, and my obsession with the art of dance and music. I know that you are looking down on me and my sister and immensely proud of our accomplishments.

To my sharp-witted brother, Jovan E. Perrin, a sibling with so many special talents and gifts:
Thank you for always supporting me. I remember you as the little 2-year-old who could shoot nerf balls from across the room and make a basket from every single angle. I am also your supporter and will always have your back. I have always wanted to be the perfect big sister and role model.

Special love for nephew and niece Michajah and Messiah—they are always blessed. (Psalms 25:4- - Lord, I pray that you would guide my children in your truth and teach them your ways.)

And to my gifted, gorgeous sister, Carla M. Fisher, who excels as a Spokesperson, Model, Actress, and Sports Commentator: I look up to you for all the great things and challenges you've overcome in life. From a young age, you were blessed with amazing gifts, and you continue to share your knowledge with so many. I love you from the bottom of my heart for your unconditional love.

Special shoutout to my "besties" for always having my back through thick and thin. These women have always had individually extraordinary gifts and values that can't be replaced or ever duplicated. Rose , Tasha , Rhonda, Tika, Eva, and Jaquie.

And my extended Powerhouse crews:
The Jacksonville Crew: Nicole, Megan, Nikki, Starr, Meisha, and Kayla. Special mentions, Delton, Trissy, Nancy, and Ann.
The Atlanta Crew: Karen, Terry, Daniel, Morika, and Shernovious, Electra.

To all my family members and the ones that are not named for all your love. The Valerie family, Aunts, Uncles, and Cousins, Morris and Char, Jacque , Marcello, John , Melody Lee, Majorie , and all of my numerous family members past and present. Auntie Carol and Crystal . Garnell and Emma . All the wonderful family members that I met at the family reunion. And so many others- Love You. All Family Friends who continue to pray for our family, Alice

For these beautiful pictures, thank you Lou Freeman at Lou Freeman Photography. Lou Freeman is a photographer to the stars, a light stylist, and a director, but most of all, she is an artist.

To award winning make- up artist Gwynnis Mosby Makeup Artist (GMMA Training Center, Atlanta, Ga) for making look like a famous movie star.

I appreciate you Deidra Armstrong for helping me create this masterpiece to share with the world.

Thank you to Aimee Andrichak for your wisdom and diligence to help me launch this book into the world.

OFS Financial Services, McLean, VA- Geoff, Cara, and Alex, always making sure we are on track!

Special shout out to Terri for all your motivation and support. Thank you, Craig, for being a huge positive motivator in my life. You always remind me to keep my eyes on the prize and to let "LJ" be her beautiful, happy, fun-loving, dancing self.

To all my mentees over the years and co-workers, and colleagues from Alaska Airlines, AT&T, Cingular Wireless, T-Mobile, Microsoft, and Cox Communications.

To my new love, the Allen American Hockey Team and my friends at Zawyer Sports and Rev Entertainment. The Jacksonville Icemen, the Charlotte Checkers, The Savanna Ghost Pirates, Lake Tahoe Pro Hockey Team and Top Tier Sports.

Acknowledgements and thanks to the Class of 1987 from Evanston High School, Arizona State University Alumni, and the NAMIC Class XVIII Executive Leadership Development Program, University of Virginia.

Thank you to the Worship Center of Atlanta, under the guidance of Bishop Elect Luther McKinstry.

For those whom I may have forgotten, your support has been invaluable, and I apologize for any oversight in my acknowledgements.

TABLE OF CONTENTS

Dedication	3
Prologue	10
Chapter 1 - The LJ Way	15
Chapter 2 - Pen and Paper, Please!	31
Chapter 3 - Three Things at a Time	47
Chapter 4 - Directions And Instructions	68
Chapter 5 - Do It Anyway	89
Chapter 6 - Recharge	105
Chapter 7 - Kill the Noise	125
Chapter 8 - Become a Futuristic Thinker	149
Chapter 9 - Don't Switch Lanes - Just Pivot	169
Chapter 10 - Somebody Should Be Looking for You	185
Chapter 11 - Checkpoints	212
Chapter 12 - Looking Out for #1 - Every Day is Christmas!	236
Chapter 13 - Giving Back & the Law Of Return	254
About the Author	269

Prologue

I was featured among Atlanta's Most Influential Women in the Atlanta Business magazine, twice.

In bold caption under my picture was my name: LaSonjia Jack. This particular media channel was celebrating women who had climbed the corporate ladder, made civic contributions, and had achieved success through multiple business ventures.

There I was, sitting among these powerfully elite businesswomen, but the person staring back at me was not what other people saw. The person staring back at me was that little nine-year-old girl ... the girl who would often drown out the noise from her surroundings and immerse herself in the synchronized beats of her favorite R&B songs.

She was also the teenager who walked into the Florsheim shoe store and filled out an application for employment, not because she wanted to but because she had to. She was the same person who worked her way up in several other jobs as a young adult. However, she was also the woman who learned tough lessons about love—that you can give your all and it still not be enough. She was the same young adult woman who lived without electricity in her apartment for nearly thirty days.

She was not just financially broke at times; she was emotionally broken too. Yet, she was the same woman who had to decide whether she was going to free herself from the bondage of toxicity and learn to love herself ... her whole self—failures and flaws as well as her celebratory accomplishments. This was the woman who gave me permission to thrive without guilt or restraint because she deserved it … all of it.

So why the title? When you initially think of poverty, money or financial means come to mind. But that's not exactly what I'm talking about. Poverty, as defined by the lack of necessary resources to meet basic needs, can also refer to the times when you believe you cannot accomplish your goals or projects. It's when you think you are not good enough to have a great, meaningful life. It also means not going the extra mile because you're afraid or because others told you that you cannot do it. Poverty may also mean that you have failed many times and just don't have the motivation to try again or attempt something new.

Plenty, defined as having more than enough of something, also means that you can learn new things and open up your mind to do things differently. You can sit in rooms you never imagined, have that dream job, business, or family life you so desire. More of the same is the same. It takes hard work and determination, but we can all do it.

My life is no fairytale by any stretch of the imagination. I didn't grow up with a silver spoon in my mouth; I grew up in what America calls a single parent household.

My birth name is LaSonjia Fisher. The name Jack came from my marriage of 16 years. And I was raised in Evanston, Illinois.

I was born into an environment where the people around me had many different careers.

I knew at a young age that my life would be different from others. As I looked around and watched other adults around me, I knew that I could have more. I deserved more!

The Cosby Show was one of my favorite shows, in fact, in my high school yearbook I wrote down that I wanted to be a lawyer, just like Claire. A woman who I saw as strong, smart, and stood up for herself. That is who I wanted to become. For starters, I wasn't too pleased with the responsibility attached to parenthood, as I witnessed being an adult came with so many responsibilities.

Food, clothes, and shelter seemed too costly; especially for one person trying to juggle it all. I envisioned a different life for myself; I dreamed of something better for myself through my teenage years, into my young adult years, marriage, motherhood, career, and even retirement (which I was a long way from reaching). I envisioned the life I wanted to live.

That is not to say that everything went as planned! The journey of life has lots of ups and downs, and I went through all of it. However, I used the unfortunate events in my life to help propel me forward instead of holding me back.

It wasn't always easy. But because of persistence and relentless pursuit, I've been able to achieve so many goals that this little nine-year-old girl was told she couldn't achieve.

Being broke is not a permanent state of being; it can be reversed, but it requires a deliberate decision to change the trajectory of your life.

That decision will cause the chains of a poverty mindset to release their grip on you. A decision that will cause feelings of worthlessness to evaporate into thin air. A decision that will cause you to take a good look in the mirror and love the person staring back at you.

You have to decide to forgive yourself for making poor choices. Thank yourself for not giving up. Celebrate moving past the pain of the past, and walking into a newly chartered course on life. It's an awakening of your inner strength and power. And it causes you to tap into your inner being and release your gifts and talents and skills and abilities, and even your capacity to accept and embrace the pain of your past. When you can do all that, there is absolutely no limit on what you can achieve.

Everything I've experienced over the course of my life, the good, the bad, and the ugly, lends itself to the person I am today.

People often ask me how I've been able to accomplish all these amazing things. My answer is quite simple—I've discovered a set of practices that have garnered me favorable results time and time again.

When put in practice, these thirteen principles have helped me eliminate self-defeating thoughts and behaviors keeping me from living my dreams. I'm able to reach any goal I set out to accomplish. You can do the same. In fact, I challenge you to put these principles into practice, and watch them work for you, too.

You are the reason I am writing this book. In my day to day, I have met and mentored thousands of people who say they are stuck ... trapped somewhere between their goals and dreams, and the manifestation of those goals and dreams. Oftentimes, what's standing in the way are self-limiting and self-defeating thoughts and behaviors. The good news is that you can train yourself to think and behave differently. You can employ these same strategies to help you reach your goals.

Using my life story as a backdrop, I will share these powerful strategies that will help you turbo charge your thinking. If you put these strategies into practice, you will reap their rewards. Your personal relationships will flourish. There will be no job or project for which you feel unqualified to submit your candidacy or find the right people to complete your goals. You'll be on the path to pursuing your highest calling in life–your destiny. You will have the power to transform your entire life.

Like me, you can go from seeing all the puzzle pieces, but not being sure how to put them all together, to finding the perfect fit for your life. As I've done, you will also discover that you have to get these pieces in order and then they will start to come together to make a beautiful picture. I can tell you from experience, that accomplishment is a great place to be!

Chapter 1
The LJ Way

I owe credit to my sons, Myles and Jahlen, for coining the phrase "The LJ Way." Ever since I can remember, I had a very specific method for the way in which I handled matters. I thought most things out with meticulous contemplation before moving forward. Even as a child, I would think about the possible outcomes of a matter before making a final determination. It's why many of my mother's friends and several of my elder relatives said I was an "old soul."

I didn't act my age, they said. But this was just my inherited nature. And when I say "inherited" nature, I'm referring to the fact that due to my circumstances, I had to assume adult responsibilities early in life, which matured me faster than most children my age.

Quite naturally, as I grew older, this inherited nature spilled over into motherhood and parenting. In business we call it "corporate protocol" or "processes and procedures." Simply put, it is the way that things are done ... or better yet, the way that things get done!

In the Jack household, however, it was called The LJ Way.

Now, at the time, my sons in no way intended for me to embrace the phrase. In fact, if I can remember correctly, they first used the phrase because I was adamant that they handle something in a particular way, and I wasn't accepting anything less.

"It can't be done no other way but The LJ Way," they chanted in unison. If they were hoping their little tirade was going to cause me to relent, they were sadly mistaken. As previously mentioned, I was very methodological about the way I handled matters in both personal and professional spheres.

By the time I was going to undertake any task or make a final decision on any matter, I would have performed thorough research, including risk assessment and a cost-benefit analysis. At this stage in my life, there was too much to lose. So, ninety-nine percent of the time, The LJ Way was the best way of making important decisions: in terms of ensuring safety and security, usefulness, and long-term stability. Now, I could have allowed my sons to believe that The LJ Way had no grounded basis, but I owed it to them to explain to them why The LJ Way was the most practical and beneficial option.

I did this whenever an important decision had to be made. After all, after being married for 16 years, I was now a single mother raising boys who I knew would grow up to become young men, husbands, and eventually fathers. I wanted them to be able to employ the same strategy when making important decisions that could have significant positive impacts on their lives.

The LJ Way was born out of necessity. It began in my childhood. I was observant by nature, which was probably because I possessed an unusual amount of curiosity. As far back as I can remember, I meticulously examined my surroundings ... people, places, and things. For the most part, I was calculated in my decision making, primarily because I had a close-up view on the negative impact of not making wise, well thought out plans. And I didn't just have a front row seat; I had to live the consequences of it as well.

There's a backstory to The LJ Way, and I'm going to share it with you. It will shed a little light on who I am and WHY I AM.

I was born in Evanston, Illinois, a nice suburban city right outside of Chicago. And at the age of fourteen, I walked into Florsheim Shoe Company and requested a job application.

"A what?" the saleslady asked, looking me up and down.

"An application. I need to fill out an application," I said.

"Aren't you in school?" the saleslady asked.

"I can work after school," I countered. I knew where she was going with her line of questioning.

She inhaled. "And how old are you anyway?"

"Fourteen," I said, confidently.

"You have to be sixteen to work. Don't you know that?"

She was correct. The legal working age was sixteen. However, there was an exception to the legal statute, as the researcher in me had already discovered. "But fourteen-year-olds can work if they

17

get special permission from their parents."

Her eyes grew wide. She didn't expect that the little black girl standing in front of her had done her homework and knew the laws.

"Well ... well, you're correct. You need special permission to work, and you can't work long hours either. But hold on, I'll grab an application for you," she said as she retreated to the back of the store.

When she disappeared, I glanced around the store. I could already see myself working there, helping customers purchase quality shoes. I would be working to gain some semblance of financial independence. Ultimately, however, I would be working to be a career minded young woman. This was the start.

Within moments, the saleslady returned holding a long piece of paper ... the job application.

"You can bring that home and fill it out. You'll need to have a parent sign it, too."

"Thank you," I said, reaching for the form.

I brought the form home, filled it out, had my mother sign it, and brought it back to Florsheim Shoe Company the very next day. My goal was to not let the saleslady forget about me. I was interviewed the same afternoon and offered the job on the spot.

I took my job seriously and worked diligently. Yes, I missed out on many of the activities that friends my age got to enjoy, but I had set myself some goals to attain.

That first job changed the trajectory of my life. At age fourteen I learned that a change in my circumstances required a change in course through action. I also learned organization and leadership from my manager.

The Evanston store is where I worked during the week, but I had a chance to work extra hours at the Water Tower place in downtown Chicago, and that place was beautiful! My manager at the time also worked there and I had the opportunity to see people shopping that had lots of money and they looked so very happy. I also decided that business is what I wanted to do when I got older. In fact, even up to this day, I always look at men's shoes to see if they have taps on the bottom of their leather soles and if they take care of them properly.

When I was about fifteen, I was paired with a girl named Elizabeth in the Big Brother Big Sister program. Beth, which was her nickname, was a student at Northwestern University. As part of our bonding excursions, Beth would often take me on campus with her. I was a sophomore in high school. Up until this time, I hadn't thought about attending college. But going on the grounds of Northwestern University with Beth stirred my juices, so to speak.

College seemed like fun. College kids seemed to be enjoying college life. I had an up-close look at what higher education was like, and I was intrigued.

I made myself content with not going off to college like most of my peers. I continued to work, and landed one of the best jobs I've had in my life when I applied for and was offered a job at Sound Warehouse Music Store. At that time, CD's were created, and this was one of two biggest stores in the Chicago area. I went in with the same mentality and mission I had at Florsheim Shoe Company; which was to work hard, make an indelible impact, eventually move onto the next job, and double my worth and pay.

It didn't take long before my strong ethic and my ability to streamline the operational processes led to my being promoted as manager. Eventually, I'd leave the music store and land another job, one with more status and more money ... just as I had planned.

That place was a medical malpractice insurance company for doctors and hospitals. Carved in a gold nameplate on my desk were the words LaSonjia Fisher. I'd find myself staring at the nameplate throughout the day. I didn't know anyone else my age who dressed up to go to a semi-corporate job and earned a decent salary at eighteen ... and all that without having a college degree, mind you. I bought a car and eventually moved into my own apartment, as things seemed to be going well for me. I was crossing off all the tasks and goals that I had recorded in my journals and planner books.

I was happily working at my desk one afternoon while engaged in a casual conversation with one of my coworkers, an older woman named Anne, when I had to face the reality of my situation.

"So, what are your plans?"

She'd caught me off guard, so I looked at her a little strange. "Plans?" I said, waiting for her to provide some context.

"Yeah, what are your plans for your future? Are you planning on going to college?"

"Eventually," I said, thinking to myself, "I'm young, making good money, and college can wait."

She cleared her throat. "Well, you know, without a college degree, you're not going to go any higher in this company. Upper management positions all require college degrees."

For the first time, I felt the sting of not being in college ... being left behind. Her words hurt. I was faced with the reality that not having a college degree was limiting my choices and options. No one would be able to see how dedicated I was and how much of a hard worker I was, even my resume and job application was being tossed aside because I did not have a college degree.

Needless to say, I had to do some self-assessment. I had to evaluate where I was on the path to attaining my dreams and goals. The experience was painful, but I gained wisdom. I learned that there is measurable value in every experience.

While finishing college, I had the opportunity to get married. As all marriages do, ours required work. We were young and still trying to come into ourselves, which made the work that much more complicated. The birth of our sons Myles and Jahlen masked the seriousness of our marital woes because our focus was on parenting, not each other. This only caused things to get worse. Why? We were not addressing immediate problems in the marriage. I found myself "letting things go" at the expense of my self-esteem and dignity. But I stayed because I'd overheard one too many conversations and prophecies that I'd be the stereotypical divorcee: single woman with kids struggling financially to support them. Since I was hell-bent on proving them wrong and fighting for my own peace and sanity, I had to make one of the hardest decisions in my life—to divorce my husband. I'm glad to say we are good with each other today, despite the divorce.

My internal struggle wasn't just about divorcing my now ex-husband; it was about breaking up the home and causing my sons to live without a man in the house. The decision to leave caused me many sleepless nights. Had it not been for my closest network of supporters, especially the support of my family and my best friends, I don't know how I would have maintained my sanity. Once again, I found myself at a place where I needed to reassess and devise a strategic plan for not just my life, but for my sons as well. I didn't have all the answers, and I made some mistakes along the way; most of which, if I had to be honest, were self-inflicted. I had to have an honest talk with myself and redefine my self-image as well as my perspective of the world around me. Then I had to revert to a principle I learned when I was a teenager —**a change in circumstances requires a change in course through action.** From that very moment, it was GAME ON!

What did I do? I became deliberate about every plan and goal. I wrote everything down. I revised and revisited my goals frequently, almost daily. I researched anything and everything. I was determined to be knowledgeable about all matters that pertained to my children and myself. And this is how The LJ Way was formed. Today, The LJ Way has served the Jack family well. It has helped me navigate some of the most troublesome waters in my life and pursue goals and dreams thought to be unobtainable. It is responsible for me being appointed to executive positions at some of the country's most prestigious companies. It's helped me raise two amazing boys who are smart, talented, and sports-driven, one of which is a professional football player in the National Football League and the other obtaining a dual college degree. And while I didn't initially follow the traditional college track, today I hold a Bachelor's in General Business, a Master's in Organizational Management, and have completed an advanced education program at University of Virginia's Darden School of Business. How about that for a comeback?!

I really have to take a moment to thank Myles and Jahlen. Even though they're not penning this book, their contribution in coining the phrase, The LJ Way, is invaluable in more ways than one. My main focus after having kids was to be the BEST Role model for them both. That is still my goal, it is what keeps me striving. It keeps the fire burning and lights my inner drive. I want to show my sons, and all of my readers, that anything is possible. Not just possible, but truly obtainable.

In my opinion, this book is long overdue. Some might say it's right on time. I've long wanted to share my story of how I went to a "Plenty" mindset in the hopes that it could help another "LaSonjia" and transform his or her life. There's no magic involved. I simply opened myself up to a world of possibilities and put in the work. My success didn't happen overnight. So, if you're looking for a quick fix or an overnight gimmick, you won't find it here. If you want to transform your life and get rid of self-defeating habits, then this is the book for you. If you are ready for TRANSFORMATION... then now is the time for you.

In the remaining chapters of this book, I will share the key principles and strategies that I put into practice to help me achieve my goals. There is no secret to success. Success is duplicatable, achieved by repeatedly employing strategies that produce favorable results. Like me, you can go after and achieve your wildest dreams.

CHAPTER 1 EXERCISES

As Chapter 1 reveals, a setback is nothing more than a launching pad for a comeback. Can you recall a setback that you experienced that actually turned out to be a launching pad for something greater? If so, describe in detail.

Do you ascribe to the saying, that a change in circumstances requires a change in course through action? Why or why not?

What is the most difficult decision you've ever had to make?

How did you arrive at that decision?

Did your decision affect or impact others?

If you had to do it all over again, would you make the same decision? Why or why not? Who would you seek out to help you?

Chapter 2
Pen and Paper, Please!

Anyone who knows me, knows that I document everything. I don't come to any meeting, formal or informal, without a pen and paper.

It's a habit I can trace back to my days working for Alaska Airlines, when I was selected to work with their specialized Help Desk. All selected candidates had to undergo extensive training which required learning and retaining a large volume of information. We were evaluated on our knowledge and had to receive relatively high scores to pass.

This is how I learned to take detailed notes. Those working on the specialty Help Desk had to know more than just how to make reservations. We had to learn about mechanical parts of the aircraft (planes), as well. From Turboprop, Regional, Short-Haul, and Federline aircrafts to Jets, Commuter liners, Airbuses, and others, we had to become knowledgeable about each of them.

Not only did I learn how to take detailed notes, but the training at Alaska Airlines also forced me to create my own version of shorthand dictation. When I had a fast-talking instructor, I had to develop a technique that would allow me to document important information in an efficient way, and at the same time, minimize the risk of overlooking small details.

Documentation is the first step to becoming organized and

turning actionable tasks to goals. I adopted the skill of note taking and documentation in my twenties, and I have used it to my advantage ever since. In fact, if I were to give you a tour of my home office today, I could show you journals, planners, and other notebooks dating back twenty years or more. I can show you how far back an idea started in my head, even before it came into fruition. I'm a stickler when it comes to documentation. In fact, I've not hired a very qualified candidate because he came to an interview without having a pen and paper. And yes, I made a judgment call based on my initial interaction with the candidate. My interpretation of his action was that, if he could come to an interview without pen and paper, he'd come to a meeting without pen and paper. He would not be able to write important details, there is no way that you can remember everything that needs to be done. Remember, first impressions are lasting impressions.

Documenting your daily tasks, goals, and other plans has several benefits, some of which have positive effects on our physical and mental health. Let's explore the top six.

1. ACTIVATES THE PURSUIT.

"Write the vision, and make it plain upon the tables, that he may run that readeth it" can be found in the Bible. The author of the book in which the statement is found was a prophet named Habakkuk who was recounting an encounter he had with God about a vision he had been shown.

I've heard people quote this scripture, but they don't quite quote the entire passage, omitting the resulting effect of documenting their goals and visions. The first part of the statement instructs us to write our visions down. Simply put, we should document our goals and dreams. Writing the vision down activates your pursuit of the vision and ties your focus to it. With your focus tied to your vision, you can see the "big picture" view. This lets you plan smaller goals that, as you achieve them, will lead you towards your ultimate goal.

The latter half of the directive, however, stipulates the resulting effect of documenting your vision—it brings the vision to life, and anyone who reads the vision will "run with it." In one interpretation this could mean that the reader moves from being passive to becoming action oriented.

Research has found that those who document their visions are more likely to pursue them. Undocumented visions (our goals and dreams) are akin to coffins—it's just a matter of time before they are lowered into the ground and covered with dirt.

2. GOOD RECORD-KEEPING PRACTICE.
Writing things down is an excellent way of keeping usable, long-term records. Good record-keeping measures maintain focus on what things need your attention.

We can get busy in the day-to-day shuffle and bustle, but when we have a record of what task we need to tackle, we can stay on top of things. Too much "stuff" in the back of our minds is like thick gray fog. It's there, but not nothing is clearly visible.

When there is no visibility, things fall by the wayside. Keeping good records pays off in huge dividends. It helps you develop a system of operations that is customized to your own unique needs. Keeping good records even helps you stay on top of your credit.

While many people tend to believe that credit issues are the result of lack of money, research begs to differ. Outside of inordinate medical bills, many dings that wind up on people's credit are a result of "oversight"—they simply forgot to pay the bill. Your brain is not a computer, and you are prone to forget.

In the age of technology, it's easy to whip out our phones and use our Notes app to jot down important information. Some people even create sophisticated documents and store them on their devices. While the idea is to document goals, using technology to do so places restrictions on ease of accessibility.

For instance, let's say you wake up in the middle of the night filled with excitement about something you just saw in a dream. What are the chances that you're going to power up your laptop and write the dream or vision down? Slim to none, right?

That is why documenting by hand is the most efficient and effective way. You should record anything and everything that has your attention—your client meetings, grocery shopping list, that "big idea" you thought of while taking a shower, your business strategies, the habits you're trying to develop, that quote you liked, lyrics to your favorite songs, important dates, etc. And, you need to store the information in a place that is readily accessible.

3. Eliminates Anxiety.

When you write everything down, you'll discover that you are less anxious. You often experience a sense of relief. This is because your brain is no longer trying to filter through the chaos of where your attention should be directed.

With decreased levels of anxiety, you are better able to put a strategy in place on how to tackle the "low-hanging fruit." Tasks that can be completed in under an hour fall into this category. Tackling the low-hanging fruit is a tactic that allows you to attend to the quick and easy tasks such as making a telephone call, composing a brief email, or even running a simple errand such as going to the post office to mail a letter or a package and permanently cross them off your list. This is a tactic that can save you time as well as mental and physical energy once it is mastered. Not to mention, that checking things off your to-do list gives you a little serotonin boost, and can help you feel more accomplished and content.

4. BRINGS CLARITY.

Writing things down helps to clarify your goals, priorities, and intentions. Clarity is important because it provides focus. When you have clear focus, you can begin to add additional context around your goals and evaluate each of them for relevancy, immediacy, and priority. In other words, ask yourself the following questions:

Which vision do I really resonate with?
Which ones are vague and need additional context?
Which ones do I deem a priority?
Which can I defer for later?

With clear focus around your vision or goal, it is easier to develop a step-by-step action plan. Once you have prioritized your larger goals, the next step is to set realistic timeframes that will bring the larger vision into manifestation. As previously mentioned, the first execution step should be to tackle the low-hanging fruit.

5. Maintains Motivation.

It's been proven that writing things down helps you stay motivated. It's easy to get bored with the minutiae of day-to-day rituals.

Even when you think you've just thought of the most magnificent idea, the motivation won't last unless there's consistent drive and push around the idea. Motivation is temporal. Writing your goals down is the first step toward accountability to yourself. The secret is, that you must set some exciting goals around your vision. The more you practice the art and skill of documenting your goals and dreams, establishing action plans around them, revisiting them, and revising them, the more likely you are to stay motivated. Why? Because you are engaged. Staying engaged is key.

I have coached many people on the skill of writing down their goals and developing time-based actionable plans to achieve them. I have discovered that when people don't have exciting goals, they are less likely to put in the work to bring them into fruition. On the contrary, those who have exciting dreams are more likely to write them down, revisit and revise them, and create actionable, time-dependent plans to achieve them.

6. Higher Intellectual Capacity.

A number of clinical studies have found that writing things down enhances your mental functioning and capacity. Our brains are meant for processing, not storing. Documenting on paper frees the brain from memory overload, promoting a higher level of functioning.

With the low-hanging fruit tackled, you can focus on more complex tasks that require evaluation and analysis. You can evaluate what worked, what didn't, document what to do differently on the next go around, gauge your strengths and weaknesses, and ultimately decide whether you want to continue to pursue any particular goal or vision.

Outside of becoming organized and joining the ranks of those who achieve greater levels of success by writing their visions, goals, and dreams down; this practice also helps you to process your emotions.

Journaling is a creative and non-structured way to record thoughts and feelings. Journaling helps us connect with our inner being, figuring out what makes us tick, what makes us sad, and more importantly, what makes us happy. It's also a way of facing our giants. When our problems stay in our minds, they become monsters that control us … our thoughts, emotions, and even our behaviors.

When we express our thoughts and feelings in written form, we often discover that our problems are not nearly as big as believed.

When we realize that the perceived giant in our lives isn't really a giant at all, we have the power to terminate its very existence.

Journaling is that powerful. And as the age-old adage states, "The pen is [indeed] mightier than the sword." ~ Edward Bulwer-Lytton

If you're still unconvinced of the power of the pen, review the list below of industry leaders who believe strongly in writing things down:

David Allen, productivity consultant and author of Getting Things Done

Tim Ferriss, podcaster and author of The 4-Hour Workweek

Richard Branson, entrepreneur and founder of the Virgin Group

Marie Forleo, life coach and motivational speaker

Tony Robbins, motivational speaker and author of Awaken the Giant Within

Oprah, media giant and former talk show host of the Oprah Winfrey Show

Hal Elrod, motivational speaker and author of The Miracle Morning

Robin Sharma, writer and leadership speaker

Michael Hyatt, motivational speaker and author of Platform: Get Noticed in a Noisy World

Chapter 2 Exercises

This book will teach you a simplified way of documenting your visions, goals, and dreams and setting actionable plans around them. The first step is to document your daily tasks by creating a functioning To-Do List. The purpose of the following exercise is to show you a structured way of documenting, tackling, and refining your goals. It will also help you set realistic timelines and evaluate your success.

Create a To-Do list, and list with at least 10 tasks to tackle tomorrow, in no special order. Take 10 minutes and write them down as quickly as they come to you.

Revise the list from above, but this time order the list in terms of priority. In other words, a task is a priority if it can result in loss of life, income, housing, financial status (lowered credit scores). Most important things first!!

Revise your list once again. This time, order it with the low-hanging fruit listed first.
You may shuffle things around and your list may look different from the one above.

*It's time to evaluate each of the goals/tasks for relevancy, immediacy, and priority. Are there any tasks you can delegate to others? Determine how long will it take you to clear the entire task list? Place estimated timelines next to each task.
(X# of days, X # of weeks, X# of months, X # of years)*

Which tasks are likely to rollover/spill over to the following day? Create your new To-Do list now. Note that none of your lists should look the same. Each day things should shift and change. If you are not used to documenting your daily tasks (which should be tied to larger goals), you may need to practice this exercise daily for a while until it comes easily to you. While you are crossing some tasks off your To-Do list every day, you should also be adding new tasks to it. A To-Do list is like a living entity. It needs to be cared for, adjusted, fed, and paid attention to in order for it to stay healthy.

Do you maintain a journal? If not, why not? If so, how often do you write in your journal?

Do you express your true feelings in your journal? If you don't maintain a journal, in what way do you express your emotions?

In what way or ways would you say maintaining a daily journal has helped you or could help you?

Chapter 3
Three Things at a Time

Don't bite off more than you can chew—My grandmother said it. My mother said it. And I'm sure your grandmother and mother said the same thing to you.

This particular idiom has both physiological and sociological consequences. In the physiological sense, biting off more than you can chew will cause you to choke, which could end in death.

Sociologically, when you bite off more than you can chew, you are essentially overcommitting yourself. In the end, you won't be able to deliver on what you've promised. And in today's day and age, failing to deliver on a promise is something that can permanently tank your reputation.

The recommendation against biting off more than you can chew is a word of wisdom that has been around since the dawn of humanity. However, it's not just a common adage; it's a deeply sound word of caution.

Survey any three of your friends and dare to ask them what projects, outside of their nine-to-five, that they're working on, or even what they plan on working on; and see what responses they give you.

You'd be surprised. Some people will spit off twenty different things they are "working on," while others will find it hard to even mention one project, goal, or business venture they are currently part of. You'll probably even hear them mention goals or projects they've been mentioning for the past fifteen or twenty years.

Sadly, most people will be no further along towards obtaining that goal or finishing that project, than they were fifteen or twenty years ago when they first started dreaming about it. The reason why is very simple—they have not practiced the strategy of goal setting, goal defining, goal restructuring, and goal implementation.

Simply put, much of what they've been sharing with you boils down to a dormant desire. The goal remains stuck in a static state or gets tossed mentally because there is no strategy in place to execute.

Most of us have experienced that last-minute item shopping at some point in our lives. As a woman, I can't tell you how many times I've stopped at a department store on my way to an event, just to pick up a clothing accessory or piece of jewelry, something that would complement my outfit. I'm usually in a rush, and of course, I always want to kick myself for being in the predicament in the first place. I mean, if I'm going to shop frequently I should be picking up accessories, too. Not just purchasing my third pair of red pumps, another black purse, or yet another bottle of the same expensive perfume.

So now, imagine the scene again—you're already pressed for time, but the store is located in the same direction that you are headed. So, you go for it. You know the layout of the store well, so you anticipate you'll be in and out of the store in ten minutes or so. Now imagine walking into the store and the store is being remodeled. Nothing is where you thought it would be. All you need is a scarf, a necklace, or a pair of shiny earrings.

You can't begin to think of where to look because everything is jumbled together. If you're like me, anxiety begins to build, your heart begins to race, and sweat pebbles begin to escape the pores on your forehead and in your armpits. You are about to be late for that event or that last minute scheduled meeting.

Now, your situation is much more dire than it was previously—for women, your makeup is at risk of becoming runny. Your clothes are at risk of being saturated by perspiration. Time is ticking ... and the list goes on. You have three choices in this scenario:

- Sort through the chaos to find what you need.
- Go to another store.
- Head to your event or meeting without the item.

Each of the above options have associated consequences. You're losing time by staying at the store to find and purchase what you need. You are losing time by going to another store. And you'll probably feel as though your outfit is incomplete for the entire duration of the event. Now, imagine just how much easier your life would be if when you walked in the store, items were categorized and grouped appropriately? It would save you time and lessen your anxiety.

As shown in the above example, organization is key.

Organization is the key to alleviating many stressors in our lives. Whether it's a personal or professional pursuit, we must establish some measure of organization if we want to be successful in accomplishing our goals.

For many, this should be incentive enough to get motivated and start working.

Organization, in this sense, doesn't equate to making sure the pantry in your house looks like one in a model home where all the canned goods are neatly stacked and the labels facing front. Nor does it mean that your closets have to be meticulously arranged in color-coordinated fashion. Organization, in this sense, just refers to categorizing, condensing, and prioritizing your goals. It's a vital step when it comes to simplifying your life and eliminating chaos, stagnation, and confusion.

Goals typically fall under one of the four pillars of life—
- Faith
- Family and Friendships
- Finances
- Fitness

Faith, in this regard, does not necessarily indicate a religious foundation. It is just your basic belief system. In other words, it's the belief you hold about yourself and what you have the power to achieve. If you do not have a solid belief system, you must reshape it if you want to be successful with goal setting.

Do you need to seek out a church, synagogue or other group to help you better understand your belief system? Your thoughts and emotions must be in sync, or no amount of writing your goals down on scrap paper, a writing pad, on a white board, in a Word document on your computer., or quoting affirmations in the mirror every morning, will aid you in accomplishing your goals.

Family and Friendships are important in your life so that you can have people who will support you, give you feedback where necessary, cheer you on for your accomplishments, and pick you up when you fail. Ensure that your family and friends are positive influences in your life. They should not weigh you down. Don't be afraid to let go or cut off those that can block your success or cause you to lack happiness or discontentment.

As for Finances, no matter what the size of the income you bring into your household, you need to make sure that you have a very clear understanding on how to manage it. Seek out resources to help you budget; and create a plan to increase your income, if that is one of your goals.

The last one is Fitness. Are you making your doctor's appointments? Are you finding time to exercise or meditate? Do you need to seek counseling to help you better understand some of the mental stresses that are now present in your life?

After the painful experience of failing miserably at accomplishing goals I'd set for myself, I took a step back. That's when I came to the realization that goal setting required the use of some sort of strategy. However, to be clear, there is no one-size-fits-all strategy. There are some similarities in approach among the different types of strategies people use.

However, when goal-setting I tell people to think from broad to narrow. What I mean by that is to think of ten different projects or goals that you would like to accomplish and jot them down quickly in no particular order.

Please go to the Chapter 3 Exercises and start your list. For the remainder of this Chapter you will be going back and forth to write down your information. It is important to remember that goal setting should cover every aspect of your life. Leave nothing out. We'll get into the specifics later in this chapter.

Once you have your list of ten goals, then it's time to employ the strategy of narrowing your goals down. To do this, I use something I call the COTEF strategy. Each letter stands for the following components you will use to narrow your list down.

C = Conflicting Goals
O = Overlapping Goals
T = Time Commitment
E = Expertise
F = Financial cost

Now that you have your list of ten goals, it's time to review them. There is a reason why you want to start with a broad list and then narrow down. The more goals you have, the increased chance that some of them conflict with one another.

Using the COTEF strategy, the first thing you want to do is identify any conflicting goals you might have. Conflicting goals are goals that are completely opposite of each other. For instance, one of your goals might be to travel more while another goal might be to stay at home more often. These two goals are completely opposite. There are a few ways to decide which goal to keep and which goal to discard. One way to do this is to identify why each one matters to you and why you included them in your list. Another way to decide which goal to keep and which to discard is to simply prioritize the conflicting goal. Essentially, pinpoint which goal you value more. You don't have to permanently discard the other goal; you can simply push it out and focus on it at a more appropriate time. In this example, you may choose to keep "stay at home more" so that you can save money to be able to travel next year. Conflicting goals don't necessarily mean you can't do both, you just have to figure out the order that will support your dreams.

Next, you should look for overlapping goals. These are simply goals that are somewhat related. For example, you might want to exercise more often but also want to spend time with your friends who meet up twice a week. You can combine these goals by suggesting that you and your friends meet up at the gym sometimes or at a trail where you can exercise together. You can also plan hiking activities with your friends. Combining overlapping goals will help you streamline your list. Identifying overlapping goals shouldn't be difficult to do; you simply need to see if there are any natural relationships between goals and merge them together.

Next, you want to look at your goals and assess time frames or time commitments around them. In other words, will your goals take longer than three months to accomplish? Longer than six months? When starting out, you want to focus on goals that have the shortest time frame for completion.

Assessing time commitment attached to goals is an extremely important step that many people miss. If you don't know how long it will take you to achieve the goals you set, you're setting yourself up for F & F—frustration and failure. Knowing the time commitment attached to your goals eliminates unnecessary anxiety and frustration. For example, if you know it will take you five months to complete a certificate program needed for a managerial position at work, your goal list should reflect this time frame.

Assigning time frames for completion is one part of the COTEF strategy but is a very important one. When you fulfill a goal and then mark it off your list as completed, it will boost your confidence. You'll be able to clear the board, so to speak, and start all over again. But this time around, you can repurpose some of the goals you initially crossed off your previous master lists.

An effective goal setting strategy requires that you evaluate your level of expertise on a topic related to your goal. Do you already possess the qualifications to achieve your goal? Do you need to take a course or do research? By evaluating your level of expertise as it relates to your goal, it will help you assess proper timelines and realign your short-term and long-term goals. If your goal requires education and/or training that will take more than three months (or 90 days), remove it from your initial goal list. But add the task to register/pay for the class so that you can fulfill that goal in the future. Believe it or not, narrowing your goal list brings you closer to having more precise and feasible goals that are achievable. Don't forget that every goal you cross off makes you feel more confident and gives you a boost in feelings of purpose and drive.

Springing into action to fulfill your goals, without evaluating the financial impact, is self-defeating. You must consider the full financial cost associated with each of your goals. For example, if your goal is to start your own online candle business in three months, but you don't have the financial means to create the samples, which requires you to pay for final sample product, the various fragrances, the different glass containers, label design, website set-up, and distribution costs... then your goal list needs to reflect any and all limitations accordingly.

Rather than have the goal to "Create your Online Candle Business," the goal needs to be broken down into associated tasks. In this regard, the goal would be to "Launch New Candle Business" And as you move forward in the next phase of goal setting, you can include the tasks for which you have the financial means to fulfill now, as well as any tasks associated with generating the income you need to finish the project.

Assessing the cost associated with accomplishing your goals on the front end will help prevent you from having to postpone or abandon your goals because you lack the financial means of reaching them. Considering the financial impact attached to goals actually helps to streamline your short-term goals (or goal list) and put you in touch with reality. That is, what you can truly accomplish.

Even if you plan on borrowing money from family or a friend or plan on taking out a loan from a commercial lender, you must consider these factors up front. That means, you should already have confirmation that you will receive the funds, whether verbal (from the person you are borrowing from) or documentation from a commercial lender.

By now, you should have about half of the goals on your list. The ultimate sweet spot here is to work on a maximum of three goals at a time, especially if you want to achieve the goal and reap the greatest possible results.

You don't want to overwhelm yourself by trying to concentrate on too many goals at one time. Therefore, you need to prioritize your list further. Just how do you do that? Circle your top priority goal in each area of life. What are the top three goals? Remember, you have already applied the COTEF strategy, so there should be no conflicting or overlapping goals. The remaining goals should all be able to be carried out within your specified time frame. And they should all meet the expertise and financial considerations.

Therefore, the only thing left for you to do is identify your top three.

Why three? The Power of Three dates back to Biblical times. Spiritually, the number three represents alignment. The number 3 represents the Triad, being the number of the whole, as it contains the beginning, a middle, and an end. The Power of Three is universal and represents the threefold nature of the world as heaven, earth, and waters as well as the tripartite nature of man as mind, body, and spirit. The number three has inherent value, as it is the smallest number in which patterns can be identified and comparisons made.

Literature from around the world often makes comparisons in

patterns of three for the following reasons:
It establishes logic and simplicity.
It provides alignment and order.
Patterns of three are easier to remember.

I am a huge advocate of sticking with three main goals at one time. It is easier to manage the tasks associated with each as well as associated costs, which, depending on the goals you select, can be considerable.

Now that you have the strategy, it's time to take a stab at it. It's just practice. But practice does make perfect … always has and always will.

Chapter 3 Exercises

This exercise is what I call Goal Setting 101. It is meant to teach you the rudiments of setting goals using a structured strategy that I call the COTEF strategy. Follow the prompts below. By the end of the exercise, you should have a goal list with three short-term or immediate goals in which you plan to pursue. Although this is a practice exercise, your responses should reflect feasible and practical goals. That is, goals that you have the ability to achieve in a reasonable (90- to 120-day) time frame.

In no particular order, list 10 goals you would like to achieve.

Categorize each goal by placing the following category next to each:

Faith
F&F (for Family/Friendships)
Finances
Fitness/Health

Examples:
Lose 20 lbs. – Fitness
Girls Night Out once a month – F&F

Review your list and look for any conflicting goals. Once identified, cross off all but one of the conflicting goals. Keep in mind (as in the example in the chapter body) that what you cross off may be added as a goal for a later date.

Review your list and look for any overlapping goals. Once identified, combine them.

Evaluate the time commitment required for each and indicate the time frame next to the goal.
Example: Lose 20 lbs. – Fitness (3 months/90 days).

Please note that you will be making projections, which may require modification. Your goal list should be dwindling down by now.

Evaluate whether you possess the current level of expertise to carry out the goal or whether additional education or training will be required. Simply place a Y for yes or an N for no next to each goal. Then add information about what you need to be able to obtain that goal.

Example: Build Website - Finances - N (Must Find Programmer)

Now it's time to evaluate the financial aspect of goal pursuit. Do you have the financial means to achieve each goal? If necessary, perform your due diligence and come up with an estimated cost. Once you have an idea of the projected financial cost, place a rounded figure next to the goal. Then add the entire cost at the end. If you desire, you can add details as shown in the example below.

Example: Lose 20 lbs. – Fitness; 3 months/90 days; N (Need trainer and Nutritionist); $1000 (Gym membership, Cost for Trainer, Dietary costs for healthier eating).

Review your list above, taking into account the time commitment involved in the goal, the level of expertise required, and the financial aspect. Now, list the top three goals in order of PRIORITY. And assign an approximate date to complete each goal. Remember that date may change, but I want you to have a realistic approach to completing it.

The goals that you eliminated should not be permanently discarded. You listed them for a reason. Record the goals you crossed off or eliminated from your initial list below. You will use these later.

Chapter 4
Directions And Instructions

If you turn on your navigation system, plug in the address of your intended destination, then the first thing it does is orient you to the direction you need to go.

If I had to be honest, I usually have no clue of my exact navigational position. It's just not one of my gifts. However, I know that if I dare drive Northeast when I should be heading Southeast, I'll never get to my intended destination.

In this regard, it is imperative that you orient yourself in the right direction. What this translates to is becoming intimately aware of your starting point. Writing your goals down, streamlining your goals, and prioritizing them as the previous chapter described, is just the beginning of creating the life that you want … and more importantly, the life that you deserve. Once you orient yourself based on your current position, you can then follow the instructions that will lead you directly to your destination.

Just as you are required to follow the directions and instructions given by your navigation device to reach your intended destination, you are also required to follow both directions and instructions to reach your intended goals and aspirations.

It requires action on your part. Direction and instruction are meant to help you spring into action and execute a plan. Before you begin, let's consider the first things first.

You must establish some ground rules. These ground rules are rules you establish for yourself. You can devise your own, but I'll share a list of some of the ground rules I have established a little further along in this chapter.

To be honest, setting boundaries or ground rules is easier said than done. However, holding yourself accountable places success or failure at your feet.

Some great methods to hold yourself accountable are:

- Purchase a yearly planner
- Create daily to-do lists (Pen and Paper, Please!)
- Perform the required due diligence around each goal
- Keep meticulous notes
- Journaling can be helpful
- Find an accountability partner, someone who will hold you accountable and give truthful feedback
- Be REAL, have an honest conversation with yourself, look in the mirror and talk to yourself if you need to.
-

If you don't want to fail, then it's up to you to adhere to the goals that you set for yourself.

Now that you have a foundation to hold yourself accountable. Let me introduce you to the idea of having an Accountability Partner. These are individuals that you respect, and who will provide truthful feedback to you. Share with them your plans for change (including with timelines) and they will keep you accountable to those tasks.

Most times if we are the only ones that know the plan, we can keep pushing the finish date further out, procrastinate, or never get started in the first place. We may talk a good game but not execute on any part of it.

Pick 1-3 people, no more than that. Then set a meeting with them and explain your plan. Have them conduct regular "check-ins" to hold you accountable. They can be a sounding board, and if you pick someone with expertise in the direction you're going it makes it that much easier. These individuals will be able to call you out on things that you were supposed to do. Now as you finish this chapter, start thinking about who those individuals may be.

Mindset is literally everything. If you want to be successful, you must first believe that you can achieve your goals. You can create this mindset by engaging in deliberate actions to develop a healthy outlook. This is another thing that is easier said than done.

Most people are under the impression that a healthy or positive mindset can be achieved by the flick of a button or a simple choice. Wrong!

Developing a positive mindset requires training. Your mind must be trained to think healthy thoughts. Without a positive mindset, you are more inclined to second guess your skill and ability and not have the willpower to push through challenges and setbacks. What your mind focuses on, is what you will tend to focus on.

But just how do you develop a positive mindset? Many people are under the assumption that you can just think about "good things" all the time.

Wrong again! That's just not how the human brain works.

You can train your mind by:

- **Clearing your mind.**

This can be as simple as removing yourself from toxic situations and toxic people. It can also be accomplished by reorganizing your living and/or workspace. Yes, that may mean disconnecting from someone or something to make a difference in your life. When you see these things you must acknowledge that something is not right and you need to fix it. The movies you watch, the music that you listen to, it all starts with what type of positive food you want your mind to have. Another old saying that applies here is "garbage in, garbage out." Putting healthy and motivating thoughts in your mind will help you continue to think healthy and motivating thoughts.

- **Limiting your exposure to stressful situations.**

For example, some people are incredible stressed out by their place of employment. If your job is stressful, you need to develop coping mechanisms to reduce job-related stress. This could include taking PTO (paid time off). Perhaps setting a plan to move to a different job, career, or a different company.

- **Establishing firm boundaries.**

Again, don't bite off more than you can chew. This means that you have to say NO sometimes, especially if it means blowing a deadline, missing important appointments or meetings, or burning yourself out.

In the past, I was forced to fulfill responsibilities associated with my roles as wife, mom, sports mom, extended family mediator, and the corporate businesswoman. Because I had a personal vendetta against failure and not having enough finances (as admitted in Chapter 1), I often overextended myself.

Sure, I'd accomplish most of my goals, but in the end, I found that I'd cheated myself in the process. I didn't take care of LaSonjia. Her needs were nowhere on my list of goals. It took me looking at my picture in the Atlanta Business Chronicle and not recognizing the woman who had achieved all the wonderful things that the caption on my image said I achieved.

I always met my goals and got the job done; but by the end of it, I found myself burnt out, irritated, angry, and exhausted. Looking into my own eyes, I knew something needed to change … that I needed to add taking care of me into my process. I decided that day that, outside of my sons, everything else was going to be reprioritized in my life. I was no longer going to sacrifice my own happiness. That was the day and the moment that I reintroduced myself to myself.

LaSonjia Fisher- Jack.
So, take it from me, setting boundaries is crucial if you want to ensure you don't get burned out or taken advantage of in the process. To help you pinpoint where you may need boundaries,

ASK YOURSELF THESE QUESTIONS:

WHAT THINGS DO I ENJOY DOING?
These are tasks you like to do and enrich your life.

WHAT ARE THE THINGS I SHOULD BE DOING?
These are tasks maybe you already do, or you need to be doing more of.

WHAT ARE THINGS I SHOULD NOT BE DOING?
These are things that people come to you for, and they should be asking someone else. Stop being their "yes-man." You must help yourself first so you can consider going back to help others once you are strong enough.

- **Exercising**.

There's no denying that physical exercise causes the brain to release powerful chemicals called endorphins. Endorphins stimulate physical and emotional responses in the body. The short list of these effects includes regulating metabolism, balancing mood, and reducing stress and anxiety. Exercise also helps to keep you healthy and fit. Dancing is a form of exercise. And it's what I do often. Dancing also releases endorphins. You can find me at home or even in the aisle of a grocery store smiling and dancing to the songs playing.

- **Having quiet time.**

We live in a very busy world today. Although advances in technology have made it easier for us to stay connected, they have also made it difficult for us to become unconnected.

Think about it, if we discover we've left our cell phone behind at a restaurant or at work, we'll turn around and drive back to retrieve it. We can travel abroad and still stay connected to our family and friends via email, digital apps, and social media platforms. For many of us, our only quiet time is when we go to sleep. For some of us, we still stay plugged into our social media world, scrolling up and down the sites until the Sandman blows the last of his magic sprinkles into our eyes, and puts us to sleep.

Staying constantly plugged in is not a good habit. You must set aside quiet time to think, pray, and/or meditate. Tap into your inner self. Recharge. You don't have to wait until the still of the night to have quiet time. You can easily do it in the middle of the day.

Quiet time allows you to tap into your subconscious, and it also lets you hear from God (or whatever you choose to call your higher power) to receive "further instructions." You can't do either if you are always surrounded by noise or stay constantly plugged into the "chatter" of social media.

- **Listening to music.**

I credit my father for my love of music. My father introduced me to all genres of music, R&B, Jazz, Classical, Reggae, Blues, Gospel, etc. Listening to music causes the body to release a chemical called dopamine that leads to feelings of happiness and pleasure. I listen to music often. In fact, during the workday, whenever I'm not on a call, I have music playing in the background. I've always felt that music invigorated me and increased my brain power. Science has proven that listening to and making music enhances sleep, exercise, and memory. It has also been found to increase IQ and improve performance. I love music so much that I have invested in two record players and all of Prince's vinyl records.

- **Reading.**

Plunge into a good book. Reading relaxes you. It allows you to detach from your reality and dive into the world of fictional characters, or the lives of real-life people. Reading also stimulates brain cells, keeps you alert and improves brain connectivity, sharpens vocabulary and increases comprehension, enhances sleep, lowers blood pressure, fights depression, and helps to prevent cognitive decline. Clearly, reading has several crucial benefits.

- **Surrounding yourself with inspirational quotes.**

Find inspirational (or motivational) quotes and place them where you can see them all throughout the day. When you read them, your subconscious records and acts on it. Place these inspirational quotes on your headboard, bathroom mirror, on the refrigerator, even in your car. You can get really sophisticated and type the quotes out and send them to yourself as emails or text messages.

I also encourage you to change the quotes up from time to time, rotating them or switching them up altogether. You can easily find many inspirational quotes online. Personally, inspirational quotes speak to me, remind me of my goals, and motivate me.

You can also utilize YouTube, there are many motivational videos and even ones that you can play at night to reach your inner consciousness.

Write your own mantra (or personal belief statement) and read it out loud frequently. In fact, say it in the morning and say it at night before you go to bed. I'll revisit this topic in a subsequent chapter. Developing your own mantra has been proven to be an effective tool to helping people stay laser focused on their goals. Your mantra is meant to serve as your functioning belief about who you are and the world around you. It helps you rewire your mind based on your functional belief system. The exercises at the end of this chapter will provide you with an example of a mantra that you can use as a template to create your own. Write it down and put it in multiple places so you can see it every day. You can put it on your closet wall, on your bathroom mirror, in the front of this book and your notebooks.

Although I've highlighted some things you can incorporate into your life, you don't have to necessarily use every single one of these tactics, but you can select a handful to help develop a positive mindset. Ask yourself, are you happy in every aspect of your life? If the answer is NO, let's change that starting today.

No two strategies for tackling goals should ever look the same. While there are some commonalities associated with goal execution, the approach itself needs to be goal-dependent and may take a different route of execution altogether from what you had expected.

It is important that your schedule be flexible enough to accommodate unexpected events.

Commonalities in ways to tackle your goals should include the following:

- **Milestones.**

Establish milestones to track your progress toward completion. There is not one "correct" way to do this. If you are unsure about how to establish project-related milestones, break the milestones down by date. For example, 10 days in, 21 days in, 30 days in, 60 days in, 90 days in, or 120 days in.

Set these milestones and evaluate your progress at each milestone. Having a flexible schedule will allow you to shift tasks around if needed. Start to visualize what your world would be like in 3 years. What will you have accomplished? These dreams can come true, and now is the time for efficient planning. We will talk more about this in the Become a Futuristic Thinker chapter.

- **Reminders.**

Reminders keep you on track. They also help to keep your goals in the forefront of your mind. You want to remind yourself of your goals, the motivation behind them, and re-evaluate them regularly. Reminders can be set up as notifications on your phone, you can place reminders in the form of notes on the mirrors and walls in your home, on the dashboard in your vehicle, or on a vision board that you post in your home or work office. You can be as creative as you want to be with setting up these reminders.

Reminders are meant to remind you not just of the goal you've set but also of the power you have within yourself to accomplish the goals you've set.

- **Take Breaks & Rest.**

When you feel overly emotional, irritated, unmotivated, sad, or frustrated, then it's an indication you need to take a break and rest. I encourage you to take a break from work, social media, and just rest. Listen to your mind and body and figure out what type of rest you need; physical, mental, emotional, spiritual, social, sensory, or creative rest.

If you don't get the proper rest when your body is begging you for it, you'll end up burning yourself out- which can cause you to not put your best foot forward. And unfortunately, it can lead to goal failure, lowered immune system functioning, causing physical illness due to heightened levels of stress, or mental breakdown. Even though you might be tempted to power through and get the job done, it's more beneficial for everyone (including yourself) if you take 30 minutes to go for a walk, take a day off, Netflix and Chill, or take a much-needed nap.

I usually put my phone on silent or do not disturb. You can even schedule it to come on and off on a schedule if necessary. We can all take charge of our precious time.

- **Reward Yourself Throughout the Process.**

Reward yourself every time you hit a milestone or achieve a win. In fact, for every goal, you should establish a reward. Doing so trains your mind using positive reinforcement and makes the process all the more enjoyable. After all, who said pursuing your goals should be mundane and boring?

I suggest the following types of rewards: Entertainment (Girls/Guys Night Out, Movies, Theatrical Performance, Professional Hockey or Football game, Comedy Show, etc.), Food (Note: if your goal is to lose weight, then you want to stay away from awarding yourself with food. It can be too tempting to resist.), Shopping (one of my favorites!!!!!!), Travel (another one of my favorites!!!!), or Self-Care (spa treatment, massage, soothing bath, facial or body products). For men, buying a new cologne or shaving cream can be a reward. Rewards don't have to be expensive, either. In the early days of achieving your dreams a vacation may be out of your grasp, but you could take a day off and visit a park or spend a special day on the couch with your favorite movies.

- **Learn to Dance in the Rain.**

No matter how hard you try, some things are just out of your control. Change is inevitable. And the sooner you accept this truth, the sooner you can learn how to accept challenges and devise a strategy for tackling whatever challenges come your way. I call this, "learning to dance in the rain."

This is not just fancy terminology; it's something I learned, albeit the hard way. You see, I've been an avid planner ever since I can remember, but things haven't always turned out as planned.

While I crushed one generational curse by getting married before having children, I had no idea that I'd still end up being a single mother because of divorce.

I didn't think it was in the cards, but it happened. I can remember the day I left the courthouse after my divorce was finalized. It had started to drizzle as I took the brief trek from the courthouse to my car. I wondered whether I had made the right decision, having permanently severed the marital cord and breaking up the four-member Jack family. I didn't know how I was going to make it as a single parent. I knew that my hard work ethic would generate a decent income, enough to stay out of the lines at food pantries. But I wasn't so sure that I had the power to keep my sons, Myles and Jahlen, from experiencing any type of emotional scarring stemming from the divorce. In that moment, I just looked up at the sky and held my hands up in surrender. It was in God's hands.

In the next moment, I felt a peace sweep over me ... something I can't fully articulate even to this day. I knew all would be well. As the rain picked up its intensity, I danced the remainder of the way to my car. Yes, I had to reprioritize some things and shift some things around, but I was no longer hostage in a hostile environment I once called "home." I'm not telling you to do something that I've never done. And just as I learned to dance in the rain, both literally and figuratively, so can you.

This entire chapter is about following directions and instructions. It requires action on your part. It's not just full of fancy words and "fluffy" advice. The direction and instruction are meant to help you spring into action.

One of my favorite Scriptures is found in Proverbs 14:23—"In all labor there is profit, but idle chatter leads only to poverty." This scripture is rooted in the law of sowing and reaping. If you work hard, the reward is great. But if you put in minimal work, the reward is minimal. Another way to look at it is, "Talk is cheap."

If you want to change your circumstances, then it's time to boss up and go after what you want out of life. One of the saddest realities is that most people don't believe they can live the life they desire. But the truth is that you can have whatever you set your mind to accomplish. I say, "Go right to the edge of the cliff and jump off!!" What are you waiting for? Whatever you need to change the trajectory in your life, it all starts today. Direction will force you to move in a different way and following these instructions will guide you to success.

Chapter 4 Exercises

It's time to put what you've learned into practice. The following exercises will help acclimate you to the process of creating an effective To-Do List, a complementary calendar, and Project and Responsibility Guidelines.

Ground Rules

Based on the Ground Rules provided in Chapter 4. List what things you would incorporate or change.

Rule #1: hold yourself accountable

List the names of 3 people. Then call them up and tell them your plan. Whether that is to move to a new location, get a new job, or start a business. Give them dates and ask them to HOLD you accountable and check in with you monthly on your progress. If you don't call them, they MUST call you.

Rule #2: Develop a positive mindset.
What new items can you incorporate into your life to help you develop a more positive mindset?

Example: Develop your own mantra. There are so many good possibilities. "I will do my best and bring greatness into the world." You could post it up in your bathroom or closet and say it everyday. Make it a habit. Or find some motivational videos to listen to on your drive in to work or play while you're sleeping.

Rule #3: Devise a flexible execution schedule.

Start with your goals/date in mind. But remember, be flexible! Things may change, items may get pushed out further or pulled in quicker. Remember not to stress. Things will fall into place if you keep working on them.

Example: If I put 30 days on my calendar, and provide a buffer of 15 days, things just happen in the world. If you finish early, then GREAT. And if not, then you won't be late!

Now, it's time to create your To-Do List. Notice that the To-Do list coincides with the calendar entries and vice versa. You can mark a date on your calendar, but if you forget to add the preliminary task to your To-Do List, you'll drop the ball every time. The samples that I am providing in this exercise are what works for me. It sums up the information from Chapters 2 through Chapter 4.

As you get familiar with what works and what doesn't, you can certainly adjust the documents accordingly.

You might find the instructional tips coming up helpful as you work to devise a flexible execution schedule. Remember, it all starts with your daily planning habits. That is, what you do on a day-to-day basis. Your task list should mirror your calendar of events.

Instructional Tips:

Create your own system assigning priority levels for your tasks.

For example:
P1 = High Priority
P2 = Medium Priority
P3 = Low Priority.

For me, P1 (High Priority are those things that must be taken care of within 24 hours. These are things that have hard deadlines and can cause issues with health, safety, and livelihood (i.e., job/income). Anything I assign P2 (Medium Priority) are those things that can be done in a 3- to 7-day time frame. P3 (Low Priority) are those tasks that can be completed anywhere from 14 to 30 days. Anything that can be taken care of past this time doesn't need to be on the task list at the moment.

NY- next year items- add them but you must complete something this year 1st.

Assign and document the due date for each task.
Document the task itself.
Record who is responsible for the task.
Record the status (Example: Not Started, In Progress, Complete)

Indicate whether follow up is required (Example: Y/No or √)

Note: Tasks that are not completed should be placed on the task list for the next day or another day where appropriate, unless the task is being terminated altogether. And because it is sometimes difficult to recall events after significant time has passed, if you are terminating a task, good practice is to place a note at the bottom of the Task List indicating the task being terminated and why.

Remember, your brain is not a computer. This is why documentation is extremely important.

Now share this preliminary list and calendar with your accountability partner. Schedule a meeting or a call to review and gain honest feedback.

Chapter 5
Do It Anyway

Renowned author, Marianne Williamson, wrote "Our deepest fear is not that we are inadequate. Our deepest fear is that we are powerful beyond measure."

If the latter statement resonates with you, raise your hand. If you raised your hand, you are not alone. You have plenty of company around you. In fact, some of the most "so called" confident people you know are suffering, or have suffered with, feelings of inadequacy. That is, doubting their own power and ability.

In the world of psychology, it's called imposter syndrome, and it's closely associated with the work that one does. So, it should be a surprise that up to 82% of people have experienced this syndrome at some point during their lives. It's negative thought patterns that turn into negative beliefs you adopt about yourself and/or your ability. "I don't belong." "I'm not smart enough to be here." "Why would they hire me?" "What does he see in me?" "What does she see in me?" "I don't know what I'm doing, and they're going to fire me." "I'm going to fail." "I can't find happiness." And the list goes on. Feelings of inadequacy can inflict devastating blows to your self-esteem, causing you not to just doubt yourself - but can cause you to develop a deep fear of success so paralyzing that you pass up on positions that you are well qualified to hold, miss opportunities of a lifetime, and give up on the love that you are well deserving of ... all because you allow negative thoughts to run rampant in your head. Talk about self-defeating!

Even though most of us need no help talking ourselves out of going after what we want, some of us have had reinforcement, in the form of negative or toxic environments in our youth, where we were told that we were not good enough.

Although I had vowed that I would find happiness in everything that I did, and I would not have children out of wedlock, and always have a job to ensure that my bills are paid; I still struggled with feelings of inadequacy.

One such incident occurred when I was dating a young man. He and I began dating shortly after I graduated high school. Most of the friends in my circle had gone off to college, and I had convinced myself that I was going to stay behind and work my way up the corporate ladder. By this time, I was earning a decent salary, and I was reaping the rewards of my labor. I moved out of my mother's house, got my own apartment, bought a car, and had money to buy all the nice clothes and shoes that I wanted. And in my mind, meeting this guy was the icing on the cake. I thought I was living "The Life."

One day, he invited me to his home for a family barbeque. I happily accepted the invitation. Of course, I wanted to make a good impression on his parents. So, I bought the cutest outfit to wear on that day. I made sure my hair was styled by my hairdresser. And on the actual day of the barbeque, I meticulously applied my makeup, adding an extra touch that would bring out my eyes, which has always been one of my most attractive features.

When I arrived at his house, he proudly introduced me to his parents. There was no doubt that he and I had great chemistry. But we also had more than chemistry; we both had a strong admiration for each other. His parents were cordial. They engaged me in conversation, asking me about my background, my current status, and my future goals. I had no reason to think that they had anything against me. I mean, He and I were both young, and neither of us were talking about marriage.

I was just about to be 19 years old and we really liked each other. In my naiveté, I thought that was all that mattered. That is, until I went into his parent's house to use the restroom. On my way back out to the backyard, I could hear his parents engaged in a conversation about ME ... one that stopped me in my tracks.

"So how do you like her?" He asked his mother, soliciting her approval.

"She's a nice girl, but ..." His mother answered before pausing.

"But what?" He asked, with anxiousness in his voice.

"She's not in college," His father blurted out, finishing his wife's train of thought.

"But she works and makes good money," he defended.

"My son, that seems like good money to you now. But you're working a great job, making very good money, and you need to be with someone who is on the same path," His father explained.

"We like her, don't get us wrong. She's a nice girl, but ..." Your ast girlfriend is in college and will be something great. You don't want to be taking care of no woman."

Then silence crept in. There was that word "but" again. He was defeated and just gave up. He didn't defend me any further. He was certainly outnumbered and outranked, with both of his parents telling him that I wasn't good enough for him.

It was the seed planted that day that caused me to doubt whether I was good enough, not just good enough for him but for the next "good guy" who liked me and wanted to be with me. Subliminally, the message played like a tape recorder in the back of my mind ... for YEARS! Yes, even today it rings in my head like it happened just yesterday.

There's no doubt that the experience was hurtful. Nevertheless, I came back from my bathroom break and acted as though I hadn't overheard the conversation. My boyfriend tried to play it off, too, but he wasn't that good at masking his feelings. I knew it was only going to be a matter of time before our relationship would come to an end. Although I knew the breakup was inevitable, particularly because of the influence his parents had on him, my greatest takeaway was this: although the truth hurt, I could choose to let it help me.

It would take me years to understand in how many ways it actually did help me. Today, I hold a Bachelor's Degree in Business , a Master's Degree in Organizational Management, and an Executive Leadership Certificate from the University Of Virginia Darden. Sometimes not so good news motivates you to excel further than you ever thought possible - if you use that energy to fuel your dreams.

We often hear people say that "quitting is not an option." But I'm here to tell you that under certain circumstances, quitting is an option and should be exercised to the fullest extent possible.

Quitting is an option when something no longer works for you. Quitting is an option when your thoughts produce negative actions. Not only should you quit, but you must learn to quit cold turkey.

What did I have to quit? I had to quit rehearsing the negative thought patterns. I had to keep progressing forward, despite the hurtful experience. What I learned in the process was that LaSonjia was resilient.

I would regroup and rebound. I had a life to live and I couldn't stay stuck doubting myself, my abilities, or my self-worth.

This brings me back to the quote by the famous author, Marianne Williamson. You will never believe, let alone, act on the power you possess, if you don't detach yourself from negative experiences, negative words spoken about you, and even negative people. In some cases, you might even have to release yourself from the pain of the experiences themselves. Yes, it's almost always easier said than done, but the longer you hold on to it, negative self talk in your head always holds you back from moving forward.

It can hold you back from submitting that job application. Applying to college. Applying for a mortgage. Submitting that credit application for a vehicle. Going for that advanced degree or certification. Approaching that beautiful woman or handsome man. Take the leap and go for it ... ALL.

Credit is given to a man named Dr. Daniel Hale Williams as being the first surgeon to perform open-heart surgery in the United States. Dr. Daniel Hale Williams was born in the mid-1850s and was the fifth child out of seven children (one brother and five sisters). When he was just nine years old, Dr. Daniel Hale Williams' father died of tuberculosis, a once life-threatening bacterial infection that resulted in death.

As devasting as the experience, it seems plausible that it could have been the reason why Dr. Daniel Hale Williams went into medicine. While we don't know for sure, we can say that it's certainly plausible.

Just as many people have humble starting points, so did Daniel Hale Williams. He worked as an apprentice and in the barbering business before deciding to become a doctor. In 1883, Dr. Daniel Hale Williams graduated from medical school. You would think he was embarking on a lucrative and promising career. However, Dr. Daniel Hale Williams graduated at a time when Blacks could not work in hospitals. So, rather than let his credentials go to waste, he opened his own private practice. He had a "Do it Anyway" mentality. He didn't let the barriers of society barricade him in.

I am a huge proponent of "If you are going to put the work in, take the leap and go for it! Do it Anyway!"

Imagine, however, if he had graduated from high school, attended undergraduate school, and gone off to medical school, just to doubt himself with thoughts of self-doubt and fear of failure. The world of medicine would not have had such monumental contributions without him. And some of them include the following:

- He performed the first successful open-heart surgery on a human.
- He founded the first interracial hospital, Provident Hospital and Training School
- He created two hospital-based training programs for nursing.
- He co-founded the National Medical Association
- He was the first African American physician admitted to the American College of Surgeons.

And the above is just a partial list of his vast accomplishments. It is why Dr. Daniel Hale Williams' story is so fascinating to me. He is a great inspiration to people who refuse to be contained by what society expects of them.

It makes no sense to go through the motions of updating your resume and drafting an impressive cover letter if you're going to let them sit in a folder on your computer, and never submit your candidacy for the job of your dreams.

It also makes no sense to work on your credit for two years to purchase a home but freeze when it's time to get prequalified? What's the worst that can happen? They can say no … or they can say yes! Move past fear and self-doubt and do it anyway!

"Why in the world would I do that?" That's the question most of my mentees ask when I make this statement. Well, let me tell you why I embrace the notion of failing fast. No one is omniscient, except God. We are all simply in this world and trying to find our way ... our purpose. We are going to fail at first. And failing at something does not mean that you are a failure; it simply means that the strategy you used didn't work. It means that you have to try something different, a different method or different implementation strategy. Failing fast just means that you learn fast. You learn what works and what doesn't.

Chapter 5 Exercises

Review the list of statements below. Place a checkmark next to the statements that you repeat to yourself. In other words, do these statements play in your head/mind like a tape recorder?

☐ "I don't like the way I look."
☐ "I am a failure."
☐ "I am strong."
☐ "I am beautiful."
☐ "No one likes me."
☐ "It's hard for me to make friends."
☐ "People don't generally like me."
☐ "People generally like me."
☐ "I wish I had a different life."
☐ "My life is too hard."
☐ "People think I do a good job at work."
☐ "Things never go my way."
☐ "I believe I can get everything I go after."
☐ "I am not afraid to fail."
☐ "I'm a total fraud, and sooner or later, everyone's going to find out."
☐ "I'll never find love."
☐ "I have too many flaws."
☐ " I love the life I live."
☐ "If I could do my life over again, I would."

"I wish I could have more characteristics that are similar to _____ (name of the person)."

What are three of my best characteristics? Write them down and what you appreciate most about having those characteristics.

Review your list, for every statement that has a check mark, trace it back to its roots. In other words, where did the feeling of inadequacy come from? Example: "I'm not good enough." This came from the experience at the family barbeque at Dylan's house.

If you answered the fill in the blank question with a person's name, write down why you wish you could trade lives with that person. Remember, this is for your eyes only. So, you can be as truthful and brutal as possible. If you're not honest with yourself, you cannot expect to grow and heal.

What, if anything, do you need to DO ANYWAY that you've been holding off from doing? Why?

Write down at least three things (or more) that you're afraid of failing at?

What's the worst that can happen if you fail? Why is that so?

What can you do to prevent yourself from failing? Sometimes, it's just a matter of considering alternate options. This can help eliminate fear of failure because you've essentially looked it dead in the eye and devised an alternate plan of attack.

Chapter 6
Recharge

One thing that I wasn't quite prepared for early on, was the need to recharge and reset. I was under the illusion that I could take a licking and keep on ticking like the Energizer Bunny.

Boy was I in for a big surprise! When Plan A failed, I immediately jumped right in and devised a Plan B. The only problem, which was a big problem, was that I did not take the time to pause, reflect, and meditate on why Plan A did not work. I was racing against my own clock and EGO, not anyone in particular. And you can guess how Plan B turned out. You got it … not too well. Most times, it failed as well. even if it did not fail completely, the results were haphazard. Failure is the perfect time to stop, reflect, recharge, and reset.

It's not just about your strategies or plans not working out. Sometimes life just happens. What I mean by that is: even as you achieve some of your goals you can … and you will … experience setbacks. These setbacks can come in different forms. In other words, you can still experience health issues. You can still experience the loss of a loved one. You can still experience unexpected hiccups in the execution of your goals. You can still experience a breakup in your relationship or marriage, or be let go from your workplace.

Life will happen. You will get thrown off track. Things will fall apart. But you must come to grips with this reality and employ ways to help bounce back. The best way to do this is to recharge and reset.

It took me a while to learn this lesson, because at this time in my life, probably my mid-thirties, I was doing well in several areas of my life. I was steadily climbing the corporate ladder, landing many of the positions I'd applied for and my children were healthy and thriving in school and sports.

I was living in a beautiful home and neighborhood. I had a close circle of friends. But there was one area in my life that wasn't going quite the way I had planned or expected, and that was my marriage. It was falling apart. Although I was not happy, and my crumbling marriage was taking a mental toll on me, I tried to pretend as though all was well. In my mind, I did not want to disrupt the family unit. I didn't want my sons to become products of a broken home, and I didn't want to fail.

My perspective on failure was twisted. I associated the status of my marriage with blame or finding fault—there must be something I had done or not done to cause its demise. As such, I wrestled with feelings of guilt and shame. Even with all the things that were going right in my life, this one area made me feel as though I was trapped in quicksand, fighting against a powerful force trying to swallow me up.

I did not have a strategy or plan on how to deal with what I was experiencing in my marriage. I did have a few close friends that I confided in. I thank God for them. Not only did they serve as the support systems that I needed, but they were instrumental in helping me redirect my focus. In fact, they even played "second" moms to my children while I had to travel for work. The team that you have around you is important while you are making critical changes to take care of yourself.

One day while sitting at my desk, I received an email which was an invitation to my high school reunion. I read the invite with skeptical curiosity and closed it without further thought. The idea of reconnecting with some of my classmates and reliving some of my high school experiences wasn't particularly enticing. I made what I thought at the time was a big mistake by mentioning the upcoming reunion to my good friend.

"Oh, you gotta go!" she declared.

"I'm not going to that reunion," I said.

"Why not?" She challenged me.

"I'm just not feeling up to going," I said.

"That's all the more reason why you should be going! You need to get away. With all that's going on with you, you need a recharge."

"Recharge?" I echoed. But what I really wanted to say was, Me? Need a recharge? Why do you think so?

"Yes, a recharge. Get away. Take a breather. Reflect. Go to a new environment. It will probably do you some good."

"I don't have anything to wear," I said, looking for an excuse to not commit to attending the event.

"I don't care what you say, LaSonjia. You're going to that reunion. If I gotta go shopping with you, then that's what I'll do. But you will be at that event," she said with an authority that I just could not challenge.

My good friend kept her promise. Over the next couple of months, We went shopping for my outfits and accessories. I loved shopping and had a knack for putting outfits together, but I was a little cautious about what clothes I picked out for the reunion.

"What's wrong with this dress?" She said, holding up a beautiful A-lined purple and pink dress.

"It's gonna show my hips," I mumbled.

"So. That's what you want it to do. You have beautiful curves. There's nothing wrong with you struttin' your stuff," she joked.

And that's when it hit me. I had unknowingly recalled my high school experience of being teased about being so skinny, now after having kids my body had changed and I was worried about my appearance. Truth be told, the reason I didn't want to go to the reunion was because some of those experiences still haunted me. I was a popular girl, but I never felt like one of the beautiful girls. Going back to Evanston, IL to recharge seemed paradoxical as far as I was concerned.

"Well, if you don't want to wear this one, how about this one?"

She said, lifting another dress off the rack.

I shook my head no. But my friend wasn't giving up. She kept searching for a dress until she found one that I could not resist. "It's beautiful," I said, once she pulled the dress from the rack and leaned it up against me. She wanted this for me more than I wanted it for myself.

"I love it, too," she said as she folded the dress over her arm. That beautiful dress was definitely a keeper.

I followed her around Macy's department store searching for other outfits, shoes, and accessories.
But that's when the thought of Myles and Jahlen hit me. "What about the boys?"

"I got them. I'll help with the boys," she said without even flinching.

I've never been able to adequately articulate what I felt in that moment. There was something she knew I needed, something I didn't even know I needed myself. I was focused on everyone and everything around me, but I was neglecting my own needs and desires. I still wasn't one hundred percent sold on attending the reunion, but not attending wasn't an option, as far as she was concerned. Finally, I agreed.

There I was, all packed up and ready to go to my class reunion. Initially, I didn't know what to expect. Even up until I boarded the plane, I still had some trepidation, but I knew there was no backing out at that point. It can all go left … or it could all go right, I thought as I buckled my seatbelt. Just as the plane cruised down the runway I closed my eyes and took a deep breath. Then I exhaled. There was no going back. I was on my way to Evanston to face my past, live in the present, and carve out my future.

Attending my 20th High School class reunion for the Class of 1987 was the best thing that could have happened to me at that point in my life.

Not only had I been burning the midnight candle often, but I had been overlooking my own needs. The truth was that I was exhausted. I was trying to do it all and be it all for everyone except for LaSonjia. Reconnecting with old classmates and partying with them along the way was just what I needed. I forgot all about my big curves as I sashayed across the dance floor, nearly dancing myself into oblivion. I felt as though I was reliving my teenage years. In fact, I received some welcoming responses from the male attendees, and it felt great.

By the time the reunion festivities were over at the end of the weekend, I'd exchanged contact information with several classmates, promised to meet up with some, and just enjoyed the warm camaraderie of being in the moment. I even had one of my Besties right there alongside me enjoying the weekend.

By the time I returned home from the reunion, I was recharged to the tenth power! Being recharged helped me reorganize my goals, including prioritizing my own needs. My stress level had decreased so much that I was happier and livelier. Everyone around me knew there was something different about me. And all I did was attend a high school reunion.

I didn't have to go to Bora Bora to get recharged. And that's the lesson I want to share with you.

Recharging is a requirement. If you don't get recharged, you will get burned out. Your patience will wither. Your creativity will suffer. Your judgment will become skewed. In the end, you won't be at your optimal best.

Today, I recharge often. Some of the activities that help me recharge include traveling, going to a live sports game (hockey, basketball, hockey, or a football event), getting a deluxe pedicure, getting a massage, meeting up with friends, or meditating.

The goal is to take a step back and away from normal routine. You don't have to go on a seven-day cruise. You can go away for one night. Make a reservation at an area hotel and order room service. Pamper yourself. Just get out of your seat and go for a long walk. Clear your head.

Some people miss the golden opportunity to recharge because they feel the time is not right. The time is right to recharge when you feel burned out. The time is right when you feel stressed. The time is right when you need to reprioritize your goals. The time is right when something.
doesn't go as planned. In fact, it is the perfect time.

You can step back and step away. When you come back to the drawing board recharged and refreshed, you are coming back with a fresh pair
of eyes, so to speak. You are coming back with a renewed spirit.

Together, they give you the power and ability to reset. And you're not just resetting your goals; you are resetting your internal channels. You are resetting your execution strategy. You can recharge and reset as often as you need to do so. Recharging is beneficial in more ways than one. Below are some of the benefits of taking time to recharge.

1. It reduces stress.
Even if you're one of the nicest people in the world, your patience is diminished when you're stressed. That's because stress can mute positive traits and that can have an impact on your interpersonal relationships as well as your coping mechanisms. When you step away from the stress by meditating, taking a walk, or finding some other way to relax, you allow your positive traits to shine.

2. It increases creativity.
Recharging ignites your creativity. You will find that your concentration level increases and you're able to tap into your creative side with vigor. Stepping away from the normal day to day tasks, allows your creative juices to flow and your mind opens up.

3. You'll feel energized.
The stress hormone cortisol makes you feel panicked and on edge. However, when you
relax, you give your "feel-good" hormones a chance to be released. Your mood will feel elevated, and you'll be more prepared to take on your tasks for the day. Laughing enhances your intake of oxygen and increases endorphins in our bodies.

4. It helps you live longer.
Studies have shown stress is closely linked to illness and death. Therefore, when you take the time to recharge and reduce your stress, you're putting less stress on your immune system and other bodily organs and systems that help fight diseases. That could mean avoiding some fatal health issues, such as hypertension and sudden cardiac events (heart attacks).

There are several ways you can recharge. Here are some that I highly suggest:

Pray. Praying helps you tap into God. It's a way for you to communicate your petition and hear from God.

Meditate. Meditation is different from praying. When you meditate. Meditation means closing your mind to the external world (environment) around you. Your main goal is to clear your mind. Many people report feeling energized after engaging in meditation.

Take a relaxing bath. This is good for weekdays when you can't go out of town. Warm water from a bath helps you to decompress.

Take a quick out-of-town trip. Go to a conference or alumni event. You can meet new people (conferences), reconnect with old friends (alumni events or reunions), and get information that helps you get closer to achieving your goals.

Take needed naps. Take naps during the day, even when you're at work. Use your lunchtime to go to your car or find an unused room to take a quick power nap.

Spend the night at a nearby hotel. You don't always have to travel far. You can stay the night at an area hotel and order room service. Being shut-in in a different environment (as opposed to being at home) relaxes you and helps you sleep better. You don't have to worry about cleaning up the kitchen after eating. You can simply place your tray outside your room and let the kitchen staff pick it up.

Rest. Set aside one day a week to fully rest. Don't do housework. Just rest. Kick your feet up and relax.

Read a book. Choose a "feel-good" book or a book that encourages you or lifts your spirits.

Color. There are a plethora of coloring books for adults. Coloring is therapeutic, and it enhances your motor skills, helping you maintain healthy brain functioning.

Turn off your WIFI temporarily. No internet means no email. Disconnect for a few hours. The world will go on without you for a few hours.

Turn your cell phone off or put it on silent and place it in another room. Resist the urge to check to see who has called or texted. Detach yourself from outside interference. You'll be surprised how much you can dedicate to working on a project or just focusing on yourself when your phone is turned off. Constant buzzes, bells, and other notification signals disturb our thoughts and take us off task.

Take a personal day off from work. Don't take a "Sick Day."

You don't want to limit yourself to staying in the house. If you take a personal day off, you can go to the gym, take yourself out for lunch, or go see a movie during the day, and you won't have to worry about someone seeing you outside of your home.

Go to the movies, the museum, or go to a play, get outside of your comfort zone. You can go alone, don't wait for others, you need some "me" time.

Take a long drive. Long drives can be peaceful and help to rejuvenate your thoughts. Open the car windows to get some fresh air or play music that you enjoy.

Buy a journal and start journaling. Journaling is a way to see what's really on your mind. There are several ways you can journal, from freestyle journaling to structured journaling.

Pamper yourself. Get a message. Get a pedicure. Go to the salon. Try a new hairdo. Get a hair color.

If I were to "stress" one last thing, no pun intended, it is the importance of carving out time to recharge. It's absolutely crucial that you don't try to compete with other people, especially people that you don't know. It's a fallacy to look at other people's accomplishments and try to compare yourself with them. You don't know their backstory. You don't know whether they pay for help or assistance. It might look like the "Joneses" have it all together, but unless you're a fly on a wall in their home and know he real deal, it's safe to not make any assumptions.

The best thing you can do is dance to the beat of your own drum. And when the sound grows muffled, stop. Recharge. Reflect. And Reset.

CHAPTER 6 EXERCISES

Recharging can be the most important means of giving yourself the boost you need to succeed. Let's look at some ways you can learn how to refuel.

Have you ever felt the need to recharge? If so, describe the situation.

What did you do to recharge? Add some examples here.

Do you struggle with decompressing and unplugging? If so, can you pinpoint why? What are some of the obstacles?

When was the last time you unplugged and for how long? What did you do to unplug?

From the list of ways to recharge, list those that you have tried.

From the list of ways to recharge, list those that you have not done but plan to do. What is your timeline?

What, if anything, will keep you from carving out needed time to recharge?

Chapter 7
Kill the Noise

Don't ever mistake "being busy" for being productive. They are not one and the same. You see, we live in a world that is constantly moving. Our social status is seemingly attached to how busy or preoccupied we are. In fact, many people fill their calendars with "stuff" to do that doesn't necessarily get them any closer to achieving their goals and dreams.

Being busy does not necessarily equate to being productive. When you are being productive, you are focusing your attention on those things that will produce a positive end result that brings you closer to your intended goal or desire. Being successful is not about attending every networking event, responding to every email or call, or even sitting in front of your laptop for hours on end. In fact, much of what people believe leads to success is doing a bunch of "stuff."

This couldn't be more wrong. Success is about steady progression. Incremental movement. But success is also about turning off distractions and only focusing on those things that produce favorable results. In other words, if you want to reach the pinnacle of success, you are going to have to practice the art of "killing the noise." Noise, in this sense, is simply anything that distracts you from focusing on your goals and objectives. But just how is this done? Especially when there are a multitude of things that can distract us from completing our tasks and fulfilling our goals. From the constant chiming of notifications on our electronic devices, to the incessant background noise in our physical world- "noise" is all around us. If we are not careful, the noise can throw us off track. It's important to avoid the distractions, wasted time and unproductive side projects.

If I had to do it all over again of course I'd do some things differently. I, too, had to learn how to kill the noise. For me, there was plenty of noise in the background. Because technology wasn't quite as advanced when I was coming up as it is now (social media was not "a thing" yet) I didn't have to contend with being bombarded by my friends' stories, posts, and pictures.

Foe me, the noise in the background was: trying to maintain somewhat of a social life outside of work, being a wife, a mother, and tending to the needs of my mother, sister, and brother. When you are juggling a career, family, friends, personal goals/interests, and the general maintenance of day-to-day life, turning your attention to "the noise" can sometimes be tempting. Turning your focus away from what you "should" be doing can become a habit that is hard to break. Not tuning out the noise leads to procrastination.

How so? I'm so happy you asked. For starters, "noise" is not necessarily all the negative energy or circumstances around us. Noise is anything that takes us off focus, which means that sometimes, "noise" can be in our heads. We focus on negative experiences or repeat self-defeating statements to ourselves, lowering our self-image and self-worth. It's a very emotionally unhealthy way to live. If you are guilty of behaving in this fashion, you need to stop in your tracks … immediately.

To get on track, you must cancel the noise … totally and

completely. One of the first things you should do is go back to the drawing board by creating a task or to-do list. These lists highlight where our focus needs to be. Then, as previously mentioned, prioritize your list. This will help you remain on task when competing forces vying for your time and attention.

Allowing unnecessary noise to remain in the background can even confuse you about what your priorities are. It can even cause you to become a chronic procrastinator. "Is there even such a word," you ask. Yes, there is such a thing as a chronic procrastinator.

Now, while everyone puts things off from time to time, procrastinators deliberately avoid tasks and look for distractions. These are the people who attend to every notification that pops up on their cell phone. They are the same people who make excuses for not crossing things off their to-do list. Show me a procrastinator, and I'll show you a person who struggles with focus and discipline.

Remember, noise is simply the distractions that lead to procrastination. In fact, having too many things to do will lead you to procrastinate. You do 10% of way too many items and never accomplish 100% of anything. Then anxiety steps in and you stop doing it al together, because you feel defeated at never completing your goals.

Not learning to tune out the noise in your life sets you up for failure. I'll share one of my early experiences with you. Like many of you, there was a time in my life when I had many things going on at the same time. I had a project that needed to be completed for work, my sons needed new cleats for their football tryouts, we had a leak in the ceiling of our home, and it was bill time. This meant that I needed to open the mail and pay the monthly bills. All these things were swarming in my head. On top of my own issues, family and friends were sharing their woes with me as well. It doesn't take a rocket scientist to guess that I became overwhelmed to the point that I couldn't decide on which task to tackle first. They were all equally important and needed to be done, but my anxiety was beginning to have a negative effect on me.

Anxiety is a very dangerous emotion because it has the power to paralyze you, figuratively speaking. In other words, when I should have been tackling my tasks one by one as I would normally do, I didn't. I began to procrastinate, telling myself, "I'll get to it."

Before I knew it, time was of the essence, and I found myself running around like a chicken with my head cut off finishing my project for work, having to go from sports store to sports store trying to find the exact cleats that my sons needed, trying to lock in an appointment with a contractor to have the leak in the ceiling fixed, and making sure all the bills were paid to avoid any negative consequences such as suspension of services, late fees, or other penalties.

You see, it's one thing to have your utility service suspended because you didn't have the financial means to pay the bill, but it's altogether different to have your utility service suspended because you procrastinated and didn't pay the bill on time. Even though I was able to cross tasks off my list, not taking care of business cost me in more ways than one.

I lost sleep finishing up my project for work. I spent extra time and gas having to search for two different sizes of football cleats for my sons.
By the time the contractor came to repair the leak in my ceiling, the damage had worsened, causing me to have to pay more money. Paying a few of my bills past their due dates resulted in late fees and nearly having my utility service suspended.

When I considered the cost of procrastination, I made up my mind to do something about it. The first thing I had to do was STOP! Stop right in my tracks and take a look around me. There was no reason for me to have experienced those losses. Had I just kept my focus on taking care of LaSonjia all would have been well.

When I took serious inventory, it was clearly evident that I was spending a great amount of time doing things for other people, allowing myself to get sucked into other people's problems, daydreaming about something I had the power to make my reality (like buying my dream home, experiencing the love of a lifetime, and traveling abroad).

I remember saying to myself, LaSonjia, what's your problem, girl? Get it together. Get yourself together!
Once I made up my mind that I needed to make sure I never traveled that road again, I got up, put some clothes on, and took a long walk. One thing I knew how to do was put a plan into action. It's no wonder I am an operations expert in my field; I look for ways to make things simpler and more efficient, and it

can't be done by wishful thinking. It requires planning and implementation.

I put my earphones in and listened to a favorite song as I took a moderately-paced stroll through my neighborhood. The exercise, the music, inhaling and exhaling fresh air, and taking in the beauty of God's creation was just what I needed. When I got back home, I went straight to my office and grabbed a pen and my notebook so I could put my updated action items in order. My mind was clear. Once I finished this task, I ordered pizza for the boys and turned on their favorite movie. I needed to wind down and relax. I ran some hot water in the bathtub, found some great-smelling bubble bath someone had given me as a gift (which had been pushed to the back of my cupboard instead of being appreciated), and put my phone on mute.

I planned on using this day to unplug from the outside world, meditate on LaSonjia's goals and dreams once again, and bring focus back on what was truly important in my life. I called it my "Love Me Day."

Today, I still observe "Love Me," days.

As I discovered, while we might not have complete control over the external forces that induce stress and create noise (job, money, relationships), we absolutely have control of our internal state of mind (how we choose to process stress). With practice and a few helpful tactics, a calmer and more positive state of mind is within reach — and it can pay considerable dividends in one's overall satisfaction with life. You must be deliberate about tuning out unnecessary noise in your life.

Below are some of the strategies that have helped me eliminate unnecessary noise, a.k.a., distractions in my life. I'm sharing because I am passionate about sharing knowledge and information with others, especially when they help people attain their goals and dreams. Feel free to employ some (or all) of these tactics in your life.

Get rid of the things that don't bring meaningful value to your life. Make a habit of scheduling a day or a few days to declutter your surroundings. Since your home is your castle, I would say start there first. Clean your office, go through the mail and throw out what's not needed, clear out your kitchen cabinets, getting rid of old rusty pots and pans and cracked dishes, or clean out the refrigerators, which is a task I don't necessarily enjoy.

You don't have to be a clinically-diagnosed hoarder to realize that you have too much "stuff." We accumulate "things" on the sheer basis of the notion of time. You will have responsibilities, clothes, shoes, friends, expectations, goals, and dreams. If you are not careful, the noise, manifested in the form of "things," will start to clutter your vision. You will have so many things in your life that you don't know what's important. To battle that, you must see yourself as a sculptor. As your life expands, you keep on carving out the non-essential things. For the rest of your life, make it a priority to keep removing everything that won't help you accomplish your goals.

Don't waste your time trying to manage distractions. If you do, you'll just be wasting precious time. Most of us can readily identify the things that distract us. Unfortunately, many of us play mental head games with ourselves, either trying to convince ourselves that our problem is not a problem or that we can manage our distractions. Nothing could be further from the truth. The reality is that for must of us, our distractions are the things that we really like, like that handsome guy or attractive girl who calls or texts, "Wyd"— short for "What are you doing?" That's all it takes for some of us to get off track by agreeing to go out for a drink, which in some cases, can turn out to be an overnight adventure.

The same applies when it comes to our electronics. If you know you can't resist the urge to look at your phone when it pings, turn the ringer, vibration effect, and all notifications off. As a matter of fact, do yourself a favor and get rid of it completely. Put it in a drawer so you don't look for it. For example, if social media apps on your phone distract you, remove them from your phone. Don't bother trying to set time limits, most of us are not strong enough to resist the urge. Don't turn on the television or log into your favorite streaming app and click on the latest Number 1 series, just to avoid silence. You risk being captivated by the movie, and before you know, you're off task with your feet propped up watching other people fulfill their goals and dreams.

Learn to grow accustomed to silence. Sometimes, you need to sit in silence; it is a way for your inner spirit to communicate with your carnal mind. But it can't happen when "noise" is in the background.
Set Boundaries. No one can say "no" for you. You have to set boundaries for how long you will talk on the phone, watch television, take a nap, be on social media, or sit on the couch like a couch potato.

Many of us are challenged in this area. We are loyal to our family and friends and spend too much time, if you asked me, listening to their problems and giving them advice that they have no intentions on following. Unless you're physically unable, there is no need to lie in bed all day. Get up and do something productive. When the sun sets in the evening, the day is over, and there is no way to turn back the hands of time to do, undo, or redo anything.

I recognize that we are all human, and some days we might just want to kick back and do nothing. I am, however, a staunch advocate of making the best of your time and talent. By setting boundaries, you limit the amount of noise that can distract you. At the same time, you make room for productivity.
Unplug. It's hard to shut off the noise, but one way to do so is to unplug. This means you
abandon all technology. Unplugging takes you off the technological radar completely to allow room for you to meditate, gather your thoughts, indulge in self-discovery, and gain introspection.

There are so many negative images and stories in the news, sometimes we just need to take a break from the outside world to clear our mind. Also don't be afraid to Unplug from people too. Those that are not positive influences or people who are very negative. Don't forget about the people who mistreat you or don't respect you. They need to go.

Start Journaling. Make sure to carve out some time throughout the course of the day to sit back and reflect on your life. Ask yourself questions like: "Do I know where I'm going? Am I headed in the right direction? What is distracting me? What's not contributing anything to my life?" Doing so will help you clear your mind and start eliminating negative things from your life. Keep an eye on how you're progressing, your emotions, and what things require your immediate focus or attention. You'll stay on top of things and avoid having to play catch up in the end.

Health Check. No matter what your age or gender is, have you had your health check for this year? Many times, we are too busy or ignore important health signs that may even save our life. Is there a problem regarding your health that you tend to overlook? Make an appointment today to have your annual physical check. I had a simple one. Skin tags on my eyelids that bothered me. I made an appointment at the dermatologist and in 10 minutes, she removed them in the office. They had been bothering me for over a year and were gone in less time than it takes to drink a cup of coffee.

Chances are that you didn't walk before you crawled. If you did, you are one special person. And when you first began to walk, you took small steps. You did this until you mastered the skill. This principle is a universal law. Small steps are needed to get things done. To attain your goals, you must break them down into smaller tasks.

For example, if you decided to dye your hair, you wouldn't just go to any random salon and plop down in the beautician's chair. The first step you should take is to do some research. Look at various hair colors that spark your interest and find the one that you like best. The next step would be to find a beautician that specializes in hair dyes. You would need to perform further due diligence and request a consultation, find any reviews, visit the salon in advance, and interview other customers or clients, etcetera. Don't forget to inquire about cost in advance. The worst thing you want to happen is to be surprised at the end of your service by receiving a bill that is twice as much as you were expecting to pay. Once everything pans out, you can make the appointment with the beautician (or stylist) and can go with a certain degree of confidence because you've dotted your i's and crossed your t's. In the end, you'll walk out of the salon looking like a Hot Tamale and feeling like a million bucks! Remember, it's the small detailed steps that get you to the finish line.

Chapter 7 Exercises

Turning off the noise in your life and cutting out distractions is one of the most valuable, and sometimes most difficult, steps to success. Following you will find exercises and a Challenge to help you get started.

Did you make your health check appointment, what is the date?

Do you struggle with tuning out the noise in your life?

List some of the "noise" in your life.

Do you have a strategy on how to deal with "the noise" in your life? Elaborate.

Is the "noise" in your life inherited or is it self-imposed/self-inflicted?

In what ways have the distractions ("noise") in your life caused you to become a procrastinator?

Of the strategies listed above on how to eliminate the noise in your life, which ones have you employed? What was the result? What are the top three things that keep you distracted and/or unfocused?

Challenge:

Day 1: Set a period of time (at least 2 hours) that you will not engage in a "noise" activity (such as social media, talking on the telephone, watching television). During this time, direct focus only on your task list or performing research associated with defining or redefining your goals. If your distraction is your cell phone or other electronic device, turn the ringer down, notifications off, and place the device in a separate room from where you are working. You don't have to turn the device off, necessarily. Turning the ringer down, notifications off, and placing the device in a separate room should suffice. Document your progress during this period of being unplugged. In other words, what were you able to accomplish during this time?

Day 2: Add another noise activity and expand the period of time that you will unplug or not engage in the activity by 1 hour. As an example, if you unplugged from social media and/or your cell phone on Day 1, add another activity and increase the unplug time by at least 1 additional hour. Take an early bath or shower. Use a favorite gel or bubble bath. Put on some cozy pajamas and put on a hint of cologne or perfume. Make yourself a warm tea, spirit drink, a glass of wine or a cup of hot cocoa. Take out a good book or watch a fun movie. Watch a favorite sports game or smoke a cigar. Light a great smelling candle. Document your progress during this period of being unplugged. Were you able to get more accomplished?

Subsequent Days: With each passing day, add another activity that would typically keep you distracted and from focusing on your task at hand. You don't have to add an additional hour for each activity, but you can increase the period of being unplugged up to 5 hours a day. As you begin to adjust to a new schedule of working your 9 to 5, working on your own goals and tasks, and carrying out other required daily activities/functions, you will begin to adjust. Do not skip the weekends. Include the weekends. The goal here is to create a habit that helps you accomplish your goals and eliminates unnecessary distractions.

Day 7: Document your progress over the past 7 days. In what ways have you been able to eliminate distractions?

Day 22: Document your progress over the past 21 days. What has been your greatest challenge? Do you see yourself continuing this strategy/plan long term? Why or why not?

Chapter 8
Become a Futuristic Thinker

Did you know that Harvard University plans 150 years ahead? Yes, you heard me correctly, that famous Ivy League institution's planning strategy projects ahead 150 years!

Some may wonder how it's possible to do so. Well, the reality is that long-term success requires futuristic thinking and planning. The proof is in the pudding—Harvard was founded in 1636 and is still in good standing, with a worldwide reputation as an elite institution. This, my friend, is not due to luck; it's due to futuristic planning, which includes goal setting, projection, and execution.

If you intend on enjoying long-term success in your endeavors, you must become a futuristic thinker. Thall allows you to provide the products and services that will meet the needs of clients ten, fifteen, twenty-five, or even fifty years from now. Many people experience defeat in the first three to five years after launching a new venture because they did not do any forecasting or predictions related to their product.

The world around us is changing, quite rapidly. This essentially means that your goals, be they personal or business, need to be flexible enough to change in order to align with global trends, advances in technology, emergent needs, and the discovery of newer operation models, or newer ways to do things.

Do you recognize any of the following names? Nikola Tesla. Walt Disney. Raymond Kurzweil. Do you know what they have in common? In case you don't, let me tell you. These three men are futurists or futuristic thinkers. Futurists are people who have the ability to look past today and into the possibilities of tomorrow, visualizing and identifying new ideas about customers, products, services, strategies and business models. In layman's language, they see things others don't see. They think about issues most people don't think about, and they use current research to make predictive actions and forecasting decisions accordingly. Futurists are those who perform groundwork that gives rise to the success of people like Steve Jobs, Elon Musk, Bill Gates, Henry Ford, Quincy Jones, Oprah Winfrey, Rhianna, Richard Branson and Diane Hendricks.

I believe it's imperative to get an up-close look at each of these successful men and women so you can gain a greater perspective on how their futuristic thinking had a profound impact on the world - in the present day and most likely, for centuries to come.

Long before Elon Musk launched the Telsa Roadster in 2008, there was Nikola Tesla (born 1856), a Serbian–American inventor and engineer is who known for his work in electrical engineering. It was Nikola Tesla's ability to look into the future and discover ways in which electricity could be utilized in its fullest capacity. Thus, it's quite plausible that had it not been for the futuristic thinking and work of Nikola Tesla, Elon Musk probably would not have been able to launch his infamous electric vehicle named after the scientist and futuristic thinker.

People, including children, all over the world recognize the name Walt Disney. There's no doubt that Walt Disney had a clear vision into the future. A cartoonist by profession, Walt Disney didn't just stop there. He pushed the limits within the industry, being the first to add sound and color to his cartoons. You see, one of the greatest traits of a futurist is their vision—their vision into the future is clear. They know what they want, and they will go the extra mile to make sure the vision comes into fruition. Walt Disney had great vision. He was a cartoonist, but he became so much more. With imagination and vision, he created DisneyLand, a magical amusement park of the likes the public had never seen before.

Disney didn't just envision what children would like, he went above and beyond. He created a mystical world imagined for all ages, races, ethnicities, religious affiliations, etc. DisneyLand became the physical representation of an enchanting world with no limits. Futuristic thinking and planning have allowed the theme park to expand to other states (like DisneyWorld in Orlando, Florida) and even other countries. The Disney theme park model has served as the blueprint for all other theme parks across the globe. Thanks to futuristic thinking and planning, it doesn't appear as though the Disney theme parks are closing anytime soon.

Most musicians, especially pianists and keyboardists, have heard of Raymond Kurzweil. The name Kurzweil is displayed in the center of Grand and Baby Grand pianos, digital pianos, and keyboards. Raymond Kurzeil invented the first musical synthesizer, which has influenced the landscape of digital music capabilities for several decades now. But his inventions don't just stop there; he is also credited with inventing the Kurzweil Reading Machine—the first reading machine for the blind as well as several other inventions that improved the quality of life for the disabled. He couldn't have achieved this widespread success without being a futuristic thinker and planner. According to his bio, Raymond Kurzweil knew he wanted to become an inventor when he was just five years old. Five. It's worth reading again. Raymond Kurzweil knew he wanted to become an inventor when he was just five years old. By the time he was fifteen years old, he had built and programmed his own computer to compose original melodies. This was the beginning of his contribution to audio and computer technology. He simply thought about the problems he could solve, and through futuristic thinking and planning, he created solutions to the problems. He did this time and time again, moving from one domain to another. This is how futuristic thinking and planning works—desire, vision, planning, and execution.

A five-year plan, at minimum, is a must. It is no wonder that many job interviewers ask candidates about their long-term goals. As a business executive, I always ask interviewees about their five-year goals. This gives me insight on whether the candidate would be a good fit for my team. I am a futuristic thinker and planner, and most of the successes my team has achieved can be traced back to that mindset.

I can always figure out if a candidate just wants to get a foot in the door, or if they can see themselves on my team past the one year mark. I ask probing questions about current challenges in retail operations to gauge whether they've done their homework on the Telecom industry. I don't necessarily dismiss candidates just because they don't have a five-year plan. Instead, I look at what I call the "coachable factor." That is, I determine whether that person is coachable. Are they teachable? Do they know something about where the business is headed or should be headed? Of course, they must meet job requirements, but I look beyond that to determine whether the candidate is even the least bit concerned about where the company is headed in the next five to ten years.

Most businesses have a mission, a vision, and an overall strategy on what they should focus on. Most of the previous companies I have worked for have a business strategy and set dates and timelines to complete them. Most are working on a 3-to-5-year plan to ensure that the business obtains it's necessary revenue commitment to the stakeholders or even to members of a family-owned business.

Let me take you back to June 29th 2007, the launch of Apple's IPhone. I was one of the first team members from AT&T to go to Apple's campus in California to be educated on how a cell works on their network, as well as how the customer will activate their device and purchase data plans.

I would say that Mr. Steve Jobs was definitely a "Future Thinker." He would bring "the device" in various secured lock boxes to the AT&T (formally Cingular Wireless) headquarters to show the executives how his creation was coming along. This product has changed the world we live in, even now over 16 years later.

You must also think into the future. The decisions you make just for today's satisfaction may change if you are trying to look out into the future. I was a part of history, and a team of employees during that time were presented with a crystal apple, to thank us for our great contribution to the successful launch. I was able to watch that kind of forward thinking up-close, and it is literally world-changing.

A word of caution is that if you don't have a five-year plan, get one ... and fast! It could be the reason you're not landing that dream job or moving your career in a new direction. If you can't convince hiring managers that you've taken the time to plan out your own life for the next five years, how will you have the ability to do it for their company? You should be able to rattle off your 1, 3, and 5-year goals at any time.

Even if you don't have a business idea as big as Harvard or a future to change the V/Communication Industry as Oprah, your goals and desires do not have to die with you. They can experience longevity and become a family-run business like In and Out Burger, Ford, Levi Strauss, Berkshire Hathaway, Cover Girl, Revlon, or Loreal.

One of the wisest men in Biblical history, King Solomon, is

quoted as saying, "A wise man leaves an inheritance for his children's children," and it has to be one of my favorite scriptures. I love it because it signifies that the wise man whom King Solomon is referring to is a futurist, one who thinks and plans sixty plus years! The truth of the matter is that you don't have to have psychic ability to become a futurist. You just have to have the desire, put in the work, and execute! Do you see how planning and preparation come full circle? Success is nothing more than following the pattern or blueprint that produces the results that you seek.

My son, Myles, loves football, and my son, Jahlen, loves basketball. They both have different skill sets, but they both have similar futuristic goals specific to their personal discipline. They've watched me pursue and reach goal after goal. They have followed in my footsteps by pursuing and attaining their own goals.

Futuristic thinking and planning don't mean that you can avoid disruptive challenges. Instead, it means that in addition to thinking ahead and planning likely outcomes, you acknowledge and prepare for the things that could possibly throw you off course. Like my sons, I teach my mentees the fundamentals of futuristic thinking and planning. When introducing them to the concept, I like to use swimming through waves as an analogy.

Advanced swimmers are like skilled futurists — those who have the learned skills and can execute them. When swimming in live water, such as the ocean, the swimmer's skill set is of the most importance. That's because when swimming in live water, waves can become troublesome, even to someone who knows how to swim in twelve feet of water in a confined pool. You see, what separates the swimmer who knows how to swim through waves and the one who doesn't, is that thin line that separates life from death. The swimmer who is skilled in riding through waves knows how to adjust their breathing and relax their body when they see a wave approaching. They also know the difference between when to ride the wave and when to dive under the wave. Essentially, they can determine the type of wave that is approaching and which swimming technique they need to use to keep from drowning. This is how the futurist thinks and plans in life and business.

How do I become a futuristic thinker? Well, I'm glad you asked. It's not easy, but it is definitely doable. There are five of my top tips for becoming a futuristic thinker.

1. Open yourself up to change.
You must be willing to be open to doing things differently. In fact, throw out your current playbook. It's time to start a new process and a way of thinking and putting it into action. This can be uncomfortable for many people who are used to viewing things from one vantage point or one perspective. It's like wearing the same prescription eyeglasses and refusing to get a new pair because you don't notice any obvious change in your vision.

Many of us need to be reminded annually or bi-annually that it's time for our vision to be checked. It's only after we finally decide to schedule the appointment and get called to the back room that we realize the prescription in our eyeglasses needs adjusting. Becoming a futuristic thinker is about seeing things differently and not through the same lens. It's about frequently changing your prescriptive thinking, perception, and behavior.

2. Educate yourself.
Start your own independent research on futuristic thinking and planning. Become familiar with the requisites of becoming a futuristic thinker by checking out books at the library or purchasing them. One recommendation is "The Future Is Faster Than You Think: How Converging Technologies Are Transforming Business, Industries, and Our Lives" by Peter Diamandis and Steven Kotler, which focuses on the future of AI and technology. (Amazon.com)

Another great read is "The Power of Habit" by Charles Duhigg, which explores the science behind habit formation and how habits influence our lives. Duhigg explains that habits consist of a loop involving a cue, routine, and reward. By understanding and manipulating this loop, individuals can change their habits and, consequently, their lives. (Amazon.com and Wikipedia)

Both books provide valuable insights into how to think about the future and the power of habits in shaping our lives.

I've named a few at the beginning of this chapter, but there are many futurists that you can read about and learn more about how to adopt this mindset. Do the exercises or challenges they offer. Document your results. Once you begin to see results, it should push you to go further. You can also use the internet to educate yourself on how to become a futuristic thinker. There are a plethora of articles and blogs on the subject. I caution you, however, to be selective about the advice you follow. Do your research on the authors of books and articles, and make sure they have the credentials, in the form of results, to back up what they say.

I also advocate watching futuristic thinkers who might be on television. The television show Shark Tank is loaded with tips and information that will help you become a futuristic thinker and planner. Investors ask a lot of futuristic planning questions of those who are seeking investment funds. They want to know whether the candidates have engaged in long-term planning. Have they looked at trends? Have they envisioned how their product or service will fit into the future? Have they considered the needs of the consumer or clientele? I recommend you watch this show and start thinking and planning accordingly.

3. Surround yourself with futuristic thinkers.
Identifying futuristic thinkers that you can surround yourself with is easier than you think. Most of the time, they are the people you admire. They are the people who are frequently acknowledged on the job. They are the same people who are frequently promoted. Contrary to popular belief, nepotism is rare in Corporate America. Many of the people who earn top salaries and are in high positions, have earned the right to receive those salaries and

be in those positions. I know, because I am one of those people, and I know several of those same people as well. You can join associations, sit as a board member, go to seminars in your field or obtain a new training to meet people who are in the field that you want to excel in.

Challenge yourself! Go find yourself a new circle of experts. The benefit in hanging around futuristic thinkers is that we become influenced by them. A person's influences can generally be identified through their behavior. This is why advertising works. The influence starts in the mind, but it ends with our behavior.

You'll want to identify at least five futuristic thinkers. They don't all have to be those who excel in business; they can be those who excel in their personal lives. They can be those who set out to achieve personal goals, such as losing weight, going back to school to obtain a degree, taking a culinary class, or taking up a new hobby. Or maybe someone who is a good parent or has great relationships. The goal is to become so positively influenced by those in your circle, or those you are surrounded by, that you start to become a futuristic thinker and planner almost by default.

Popular thought suggests that we become the sum of the five people we spend the most time with. So spend time with people who are passionate about the future. Observe them from both near and far. Interview them, if you have to. Moreover, follow their sage advice on how to become a futuristic thinker.

4. Don't accept the status quo.
Refuse to accept that change is slow. The reality is that change can happen overnight. Just think about when tragedy strikes, God forbid. Your life can change in the blink of a moment. The same thing can happen for the good. I'm not talking about if you win the lotto. The more you prepare for change the quicker the change will come to pass.

Hard work is undoubtedly a part of the equation, refusing to accept things as they are is the hallmark of being a futuristic thinker. You look past what is and focus on "what could be." This is why Abraham Lincoln infamously said, "The best way to predict your future is to create it." There's nothing incorrect about what the 16th president of the United States said centuries ago. It held truth then, and it still holds true today.

5. Stay focused.
We have a lot of distractions around us daily. We can't watch our favorite television show or even watch a video on social media without being bombarded with advertisements on things that are supposed to make us feel important, special, or even appear more attractive. It's alluring and seducing.

But none of it comes without a price, and the price tag is huge. You can go into debt chasing these types of dreams. The highest price you'll pay, however, is losing focus on what is important.

The truth is that you probably already have a closet full of trendy apparel, half of which you can't even wear in a year's time. Your house or apartment is probably fully furnished, and you're probably driving a luxury vehicle.

Or take those three examples and reverse them, you don't have any of it and you're trying to attain that type of life- that won't happen overnight either.

Becoming a futuristic thinker requires you to stay focused. Some people say, "Keep the main thing the main thing." Interpreted, it means stay focused. Do not get off track. Stay on task, no matter what. Do not allow yourself to become easily distracted by shiny things or empty words and promises. Actions speak louder than words, so stay committed to your actions. Stay the course, and I promise you that the moment will come that you can plan a trip the day before, shop in an expensive clothing store, walk into a dealership and purchase your dream vehicle with CASH, or buy your dream home. These things are temporal, however. The most valuable commodity is the pursuit of happiness. And when you think and plan ahead, its attainment is inevitable. See It, Live It and Breath it!

I hope that this chapter provides you with greater insight and clarity on achieving your goals and dreams. It takes work, yes, but there's nothing better than setting a goal and chasing it down. If I can leave you with one last thing on this topic, it would be … "Never fear the future." You see, I love the future … it is where I live!

Chapter 8 Exercises

Futuristic thinking is about more than just daydreaming. Futuristic thinking is creating a future that you WANT to live in, and are motivated to make happen. Dreaming is good, but living your dreams is AMAZING.

Name a futuristic thinker that you would like to research, and write at least a paragraph on why this person's work interests you.

List at least 2 projects/plans or endeavors that you are currently working on.

Are there any identifiable patterns you can anticipate in these projects/plans over the next 1 to 3 years?

What will these projects or plans look like in 5 years?

Which of these 5 exercises do you think you will have the most difficulty implementing? Explain why.

Which of the 5 exercises do you think you will have the least difficulty implementing? Explain why.

Chapter 9
Don't Switch Lanes - Just Pivot

According to the U.S. Department of Transportation, improper lane changes are one of the leading causes of accidents. An improper lane change is typically caused when a driver changes lanes without looking or does not use the proper signal. Making improper lane changes can cause serious accidents and can even lead to death.

Here are some statistics related to improper lane changes:

- 9-percent of all accidents in the United States are caused by reckless lane changes.
- Many of these accidents are caused by motorcyclists.
- Almost 35,000 people are injured per year in the United States from unsafe lane changes.
- Nearly 6,000 people die each year in the United States due to unsafe lane changes.

In many regards, pursuing your goals and dreams can be akin to driving a vehicle. Just as it is important not to make improper lane changes when driving a car, it's just as important to not make lane changes prematurely when pursuing your goals. Sometimes, however, you have no choice but to change lanes due to unforeseen forces in life. This requires you to be flexible in your thinking and planning. This is why it is important to become a futuristic thinker, because futuristic thinking and planning prepare you for change, even when it is sudden. Unforeseen events in our lives can sometimes cause us to have to temporarily shift lanes- which reminds me of a recent experience I had.

I usually schedule my health-related checkups at the beginning of the year. I traveled much of January, but I managed to get a dentist appointment the next month. I was tired after traveling for business earlier in the week. I rolled out of bed that Saturday morning, took a shower, got dressed, and headed toward the dentist's office. As I normally do, I listened to my favorite Sirius radio station as I drove. While on the expressway, I noticed my car began to shift toward the right side of the lane. I tried to maneuver the wheel in the opposite direction, and that's when my car began to drive as though I was on a bumpy road. By this time, I had figured out that I had a flat tire. I slowed my speed and carefully moved into the far-right lane. I drove this way until I could get to the next exit.

When I got off the expressway I found a nearby parking lot where I could inspect the car. Once in a safe area, I parked my vehicle and began to inspect it. Low and behold, a flat tire indeed! I had two options—I could get back in my car, call roadside service and miss my dentist appointment, or I could search for the closest tire or mechanic shop and take my chances driving on the flattened tire.

While one option was safe and the other risky, I decided on the riskier option. I did a quick search in Google Maps and located a nearby tire shop. I got back in my vehicle and drove a quarter of a mile to the tire facility. I was able to replace the tire and still had time to make it to my dentist appointment. And even though I had every right to be frazzled, I didn't.

I've learned over the course of the years that you must stay the course. You see, just as in the scenario above, life itself is unpredictable, but you must stay on the right path. Even if you have to change lanes permanently or temporarily, you must develop the critical skills to pivot and get back in your lane.

Take it from me, the experience of life is fluid and ever changing. We may have our daily routines, but at some point, the monotony of daily living can and will change without warning. How do you navigate throughout the changes in life? What is it that constitutes a "changing of lanes" in your everyday journey? There are a few parallels that can be drawn from the concept of changing lanes while driving.

How to handle a change in route - Regroup and get back on course!

When you need to make a turn or exit the freeway it requires you to change lanes. Changing lanes must be done with caution. Decreasing your speed and checking your rearview and side view mirrors helps you safely change lanes. Sometimes, however, you can make a mistake and make a wrong turn or get off on the wrong exit. Doing so is enough to make anyone frazzled, but rather than stay frustrated, the best thing to do is regroup and get back on course.

This sort of reminds me of a situation that occurred in my life about fifteen or so years ago. When I was working in Seattle for T-Mobile, AT&T had put in a request with the federal government to acquire T-Mobile. One of their major headquarters was going to be in Atlanta, where I had previously lived. I thought it would be a good opportunity for me, so I took the chance and submitted my request for a new position back in Atlanta as the Regional Director Retail for the Georgia/Tennessee region. I interviewed and got the position. In this role, I drove initiatives and oversaw market-level retail performance for 80+ retail store locations in the Georgia and Tennessee region, which included Alabama, Kentucky, and South Carolina. I also had the opportunity to effectively lead a Team of 8 District Managers and 850 store employees. The role was a great one, and I learned so much and worked with employees of all races, ethnicities, and cultures. But not even eight months later, T-Mobile decided not to merge with AT&T, causing the position to be dissolved. So, to avoid being jobless, I had to "change lanes" and make yet another adjustment to my route. I headed back to Seattle.

Even in our daily lives, we must anticipate changes in the course of direction. This means, we are aware of the path that our life is taking and adjust accordingly. Although the opportunity was short lived, I do not regret for a moment taking advantage of that opportunity to learn and grow. Had I not applied for the job, I probably wouldn't be where I am today. One thing I learned over the years is that you cannot become complacent in your thinking. Life is about progression, and as a futuristic thinker, you must be flexible in thought and action, taking advantage of opportunities that fall in your lap suddenly. It's not that you can't change lanes, but you must do so with caution.

The route that we are currently traveling is not necessarily the same route we will be on forever. Life changes, and when that happens we must also change our position and direction.

Avoid obstacles in the road.

Sometimes you see it from a distance, and at other times, you don't see it until you're right up on it—road debris. Chunks of danger right in your path! You change lanes quickly, hoping to avoid popping a tire or hitting another vehicle. If you're like me, you even change lanes to avoid driving behind tractor trailers or construction vehicles. Tire peelings from tractor trailer tires are often on the expressway, causing drivers to make sudden lane changes. Debris can contain nails and other foreign objects that can cause you to have a flat tire.

Bumpy roads and potholes can also cause damage to your vehicle if you don't change your position. In life, these forms of obstacles in the road come in various disguises. Debris may come in the form of unexpected loss, be it a family member or close friend or even the loss of a job. As previously stated, you can sometimes see these things from afar, such as in the case of a terminally ill person.

Then, there are times when loss is sudden, and you are forced to make changes in your life accordingly. The objective in this case is to make the mentally accept and embrace that your life will undergo change, which will help you adjust in the long run.

Debris can also come in the form of toxic relationships. You usually see these people headed your way. Sometimes, we even invite them into our lives ourselves. You know they were toxic ten years prior, which means that they are probably still toxic when they come back smiling in your face.

Yes, I know people can change, but the older people are, the more resistant to character change they become. What you see is usually what you get, nothing more, nothing less. It's up to each of us to avoid debris and bad roads at all costs … before it costs us headache and heartache. Once you determine that something in your life has the potential to impede your progress, you must change your position to maintain a clear and safe passage.

Many years ago, I worked with someone who I believed was my friend. She would go out to events with some of my other girlfriends, join us for concerts, or we would just hang out at someone's house on the weekend. But after a couple of months, I quickly learned that she was not a very nice person. She spent lots of her conversation being very negative about everyone. In fact, it got to the point that we didn't want to invite her out anymore because it just brought your energy level down.

I would try to change the subject or get her to talk about something positive in her life, but she just couldn't. She had circumstances in her past life that were not good. I am not a doctor, but I believe that when you are still suffering from anger and pain about things that happened in your past, then you need to seek some counseling or treatment. Otherwise you will continue to focus on that instead of what you can do for your future. I did try to offer some advice, but it was not received very well and we are no longer friends. We all have bumps in the road, but we must take time to deal with them and move around them.

Check your blind spot.

Although you can see other vehicles using your sideview mirrors, and today's sophisticated vehicles have sensors that alert you of an approaching vehicle, you should always check your blind spot. Not checking one's blind spot while driving has led to many accidents. Checking your blind spot allows you to see things that are out of your normal vision.

Checking your blind spot in life is not limited to what you can see yourself. Checking your blind spot can also mean consulting someone else for their opinion and advice. They may be able to "see" or pinpoint things in your life that can be slowing you down or taking you off course. Checking your blind spot also means that you should be on the lookout for your haters. Although I don't like to give "haters" any attention in my life, the fact of the matter is that haters exist. They can come in the form of an acquaintance, sneaking up beside you, just outside of your peripheral vision, waiting for the perfect opportunity to strike, causing havoc in your life.

This is why it's important to check your blind spot before making changes to your goals or direction. When at all possible, make calculated decisions of the best time to make a change. Having patience and waiting until the path is clear is of utmost importance when considering moving to the next stage in your life. Sometimes it is better to keep your circle small when you're working on a project until it's ready to be launched to the world. That will keep unnecessary outside chatter from taking you off your path.

Use your signal.

The signal feature was developed to alert other drivers that you intend to make a specific directional lane change, left or right. In your life, this analogy simply means that there are others that should be made aware of upcoming changes that you are expecting to undergo or experience.

Your goals and dreams are not meant to be kept under lock and key like ancient pirate booty! In fact, I am a staunch advocate of sharing your goals with an accountability partner. Someone, besides you, should know about your goals. There are so many times I was led to the proper resources to move ahead because I shared my goals and intentions with someone.

You see, we are all connected in some form or fashion. It's simply only a matter of time before we are aligned with the right people and the right resources. No one achieves success by themselves, I don't care who they are. They received assistance from someone else, and they were able to get the help they needed because they shared their goals and dreams—they used their signal.

When you decide that you no longer want to change lanes while driving your vehicle you simply turn off your signal. In life, you need to notify others of your intention to stay your course. Don't worry about having to provide some elaborate explanation. It's perfectly fine to say, "I am not going in that direction or right now," or "I have decided to do things differently." And you can say it with a smile. You are the driver in your life; you are in control of your future and what happens, for the most part. Sure, some things will take you by surprise, but when you follow the "rules of the road," you are more likely to avoid accidents, debris and potholes, and reach your destination safely.

As most of us learned in Driver's Ed, following the rules of the road saves lives and saves money. Not following the rules of the road can cause accidents, where you can unintentionally injure yourself or someone else. Flashing blue lights behind your vehicle often indicates that you failed to obey the rules of the road, which can end up costing you lost time by having to attend traffic court and lost money by having to pay a fine. The rules of the road parallel the rules of life in many ways. Not following the above rules in your life equates to lost time and money, which can make it take longer to reach your goals. It is important to be deliberate in your intentions and actions so you can make a transition to the next stage of life.

CHAPTER 9 EXERCISES

Learning to pivot gives you more maneuverability with your future. When you are on a set course and refuse to change, you may not get to the destination you desire. Flexibility and adapting to change are valuable tools that every person needs to achieve their greatest success.

When driving, have you ever had to change lanes quickly? If so, what was the result?

When pursuing your goals, have you ever had to change your course? What was the result?

Describe your strategy of dealing with sudden lane changes in life. If you don't currently have one, create one and describe it here.

Is there anything that you think could cause you to change your goals or your course in pursuit of your goals?

Have you ever been challenged or questioned about having to make a sudden or unexpected lane change in your life? If so, explain the situation and the outcome.

Have you ever been challenged or questioned about having to make a sudden or unexpected lane change in your life? If so, explain the situation and the outcome.

Chapter 10
Somebody Should Be Looking For You

Somebody should be looking for you in some facet of your life. Whether it's for your gifts or talents, your genius, or because you touched their life in such a meaningful way. If you're living your life and nobody's reaching out to you or searching for you, then you need to take a serious inventory of yourself and perhaps ask yourself why.

On the contrary, if someone is looking for you, what are they trying to get in touch with you for? Is it your knowledge? Your wisdom? Is it to fill a position at some company organization? Is it because of your unique skill or gifting? Is a past love interest trying to link back up with you because you impacted their life forever?

I've dedicated the first nine chapters of this book explaining the principles of goal planning and execution to living a fulfilled life. There is no magic involved in the process whatsoever. The truth is that goal setting, planning, and execution takes discipline, hard work, and patience. Nothing happens overnight, and wishful thinking won't ever cause your goals and dreams to manifest themselves by magic.

So, just who should be looking for you? Do you cook well? Sew well? Style hair well? Write well? Know how to balance a checkbook with precision and accuracy? Know how to paint well? Fix your own car when you have trouble? Make a person laugh? Put a smile on someone's face? Encourage and speak life to people who are sad and depressed?

Sometimes, we fail to realize the importance of some of our daily tasks, ones that we might even consider to be mundane. We take our ability to perform certain tasks with relative ease for granted, not realizing that someone somewhere could probably use our assistance or expertise. Instead of taking these things for granted, we should think about how we could capitalize on our strengths, or the things that we do really well.

Unbeknownst to us, our greatest contribution to the world is not all the things we do for ourselves; our greatest contribution to the world is the value we add to the rest of the world. This equates to the sharing of our time, talents, and resources. In return, we are divinely rewarded by calls to be of greater service. Greater callings. Greater pay. Greater benefits. This is what living life with purpose is all about.

Now someone somewhere should be looking for you. Whether that is professional in nature— you're the best cake maker, a great writer, or you organize well. You might be able to look at processes and pinpoint where improvement is needed. Do you play a sport well? Do you play the piano like Liberace? You get the point. At some point in your life, your name should be circulating somewhere, and someone should hear about you.

We often quote the phrase, "I'm in the job market," which equates to "I'm looking for a job." However, when your reputation precedes you, your name is out there, and the job is looking for you! Someone needs the knowledge or skill you have. This is not to say that you don't have to actively search for a job. What it does mean is that you shouldn't have to spend hours upon hours on online portals looking for a job that millions of others are trying to land as well.

With all manner of good intentions, we begin our search. If we're trying to land a job as a business analyst, we key in the term and begin the search. If we're trying to land a job as a web developer, we look that up, and down the rabbit hole we go. If we're vying for a job as a teacher, we might take a little different approach by going to the website of the Board of Education of a certain city or county and search for the open jobs for English, Math, Science, or History teachers. This way is time consuming and is what causes fatigue when looking for employment.

This fatigue comes because we are searching for "it" instead of letting "it" search for us.

If you set yourself up correctly (from initial goal setting, to completing your daily tasks, to full-scale goal and task execution) someone, somewhere will be looking for you.

"Well, how do you know, LaSonjia?" Glad you asked. Let me show you how it's done. Here's an illustrative example of what it looks like when someone is looking for you.

Carl is the Vice President of Premiere Ad Group, one of the largest advertising agencies in the country. His advertising director resigned, having accepted a senior director role with a competing firm. It happened right in the middle of one of Premier

Ad Group's most high-visibility campaigns for one of its top investment banking clients, and Carl needs the position filled, like, yesterday!

Because we're not "supposed" to let people see us sweat, Carl hasn't expressed his fear and frustration with the slow pace of his company in vetting potential candidates for first-round interviews. His mounting anxiety is spilling over into other areas of his life.

Watch how things unfold one Friday afternoon while Carl is having lunch his golf buddy, Greg. Pay close attention to how you can be the topic of discussion without even being present.

"Everything all right?"

"What do you mean?" Carl said, scanning the menu once again.

"I'm asking you if everything is alright with you."

"It's good. I mean, it's great."

"You sure?"

"Of course, I'm sure," Carl said, looking up from the menu and now over at Greg. "Why did you ask?" he continued, nervously taking a sip of water.

"Because you usually order your infamous glass of Vodka and tonic, before you can sit down good. You haven't looked up from the menu since the waitress handed it to you."

Shaking his head. "Yeah, you're right. I'm under the gun at work. Ever since Patrice resigned, things have been so hectic at work. It's even spilling over into home life. Poor Tammy, I've been so on edge, snapping at her left and right," Carl confessed.

"Look, buddy. As one of my favorite authors and motivational speakers always said, 'There's a solution to every problem,'" Gregg said as he leaned in over the table.

"You believe all that mumbo jumbo?"

"Mumbo jumbo? Have you ever heard him speak or read any of his books?"

"Greg, I don't have time to read, especially not these days."

"You're doing yourself a big disservice by not reading or even believing, for that matter. Look at it this way. You need something, right?"

"Yes, I do," Carl admitted.

"And what is it that you need?"

"I need a kick-ass ad director. Why? Do you know somebody?"

"As a matter of fact, I do."

"Greg, you're in pharmaceutical sales, not product advertising. I need someone who-"

"Ahh ha! That's where you're wrong. I'm in business, and it doesn't matter which industry. You need someone with a particular set of skills. And I happen to know someone who can determine the target market for our campaigns, develop a top-notch messaging strategy, evaluate the overall effectiveness of all programs and campaigns, and roll out a turnkey marketing-in-a-box program for customization by branch level investment bankers in a new B2C line of business."

Carl's eyes grew wide. "Wow! That's exactly what I'm looking for … at least for starters. I need someone who can jump right in and pick up where my last person left off. So … who is this person?"

"Her name is Lisa. Lisa Mason. We used to work at the same company. Last I heard, she was kickin' ass at Cigna."

"Microsoft, huh? Do you know what it's gonna take us to get her from Cigna?"

"You never know until you ask," Greg said, smiling.

"Well, how can I get in touch with her?"

"Easy, let my fingers do the walking," Greg said, pulling his cell phone from his back pocket. "Thanks to my good ole friend named LinkedIn," you can send her a message right now," as he searched for "Lisa" on the LinkedIn platform. "And booyah! Here she is," Greg continued, turning the front of his cell phone around to showcase the name and information to Carl. This is the person who can fill the open position you have on your team."

"I'll contact her," Carl said, retrieving his own cell phone from his back pocket.

A month later, the two men met again for lunch after their golf match.

"Any follow up on Lisa?"

"I contacted her that day, and she said she was open to a new opportunity. We flew her in the next week for an interview. We Zoomed the second interview because our team pretty much knew that we wanted her. She was exactly what we were looking for. We made her an offer, and she accepted. She starts in two weeks," Carl said with a big smile.

"See, that mumbo jumbo works after all," Greg teased.

"Thank you. You saved my life!"

"In more ways than one," Greg added. "Now, your wife won't be divorcing you."

The two men shared a moment of congenial laughter.

The example provided in the vignette above happens more often than you think. It doesn't occur by happenstance; it plays out that way because your reputation has preceded you. It happens when you've put in the work and set yourself up to cause your name to come up in circles, even when you are not present. It happens when you establish goals, plan accordingly, and execute in like fashion.

Again, I think I need to reiterate that it has nothing to do with "magic" or perceived magic. The only "magic" that comes into play is the magic that is performed by the sweat of your brow. Your labor, integrity, and devotion turn into the equity that you can build up in various areas of your life. This is the formula for success. And once you learn and master it, teach it to your children, your grandchildren, your friends and associates, every person you come into contact with. It's repeatable, like the scientific method. If the steps are followed, the results will be duplicated. And there are no ifs, ands, or buts about it!

In fact, let me share with you how both of my sons' names have been circulated or mentioned in rooms outside of their presence.

My son is still in the process of finishing college, which included ending nearly four years of playing basketball at the collegiate level. My youngest son, Jahlen, has been working on his aspirations and dreams. One morning over breakfast, I said to him, "Jahlen, so what is it that you want to do during the summer break?"

"Hold that thought, Mom. I'll be right back," Jahlen said as he politely excused himself from the kitchen island where we were eating. He raced upstairs, and when he came back into the kitchen, he was holding a pen and a notebook (re: Chapter 2 - Pen and Paper, Please!). I smiled. I no longer have to remind him to get a pen and paper; he gets it and is programmed to take notes and document his goals. He realizes the importance of recording these types of conversations. First and foremost, he uses it to remember the conversation. Second, he uses it as a blueprint to help plan the execution strategy. He is familiar with not just the protocol itself but the results it garners as well.

Long story short, our so-called quick bite to eat for breakfast turned into a full-scale strategy and planning session. Nearly four hours later, we were ordering lunch from one of our favorite restaurants via Uber Eats. By the end of our strategy session, we had goals and detailed plans in place. We had made a list of people with whom we knew we had to schedule meetings with, identified locations to hold his camps, places to visit to tour fitness centers and athletic camps, and began creating a training and camp weekly schedule for kids ages 5 to high school.

Several months later, while in the middle of deciding on what land we were going to build Jahlen's summer sports camp. Jahlen received a phone call with an offer to go to another college in GA to finish up his studies.

His name was in circulation, being mentioned to attend a camp that will have college recruiters. This opportunity changed the game plan. We had to immediately put our current plans on pause. It turned out well because he started to book his flights for the camp and was able to meet some great coaches and landed an opportunity to attend a different college that was closer to home. How's that for ya? The proof is always in the pudding.

Now he is in his second year and final year playing basketball and yes, he did complete his summer camp. If the story I've just shared with you is not enough to convince you that the formula for success is duplicable, let me share another story with you.

Say the name Myles Jack, and most people think Jacksonville Jaguars and the Pittsburgh Steelers. But before he was signed to either of these teams, he was heavily recruited by collegiate sports recruiters. I can't describe the amount of mail we received during this period. Myles was heavily recruited by colleges all over the country when he was in high school. I had to literally step over the amounts of mail at our doorstep and purchase plastic storage boxes just to accommodate the volume of mail that was being delivered daily.

It's expected that once athletes perform at a certain level, that they are heavily recruited. But the wonder of the entire experience is that Myles's name was in constant circulation. He was being recruited by colleges and universities that he'd never even heard of. The beauty of it all, is that his dedication and hard work gave Myles many options in which to choose from. After all the meetings in which Myles's name was being mentioned and his record being considered, the vetting, meetings upon meetings upon meetings, tours of colleges and universities, (did I mention meetings?), and reviewing recruiting offers, Myles had to make a single choice on which to attend college. Collectively, we made a choice. He would attend UCLA.

At age five, Myles knew he wanted to play professional football. He couldn't quite articulate it, but he told me when he was just five years old that he wanted to play football. I credit my ex-husband for planting the seed for the love of sports in both of our sons. They'd watch sports with him, one sitting on his lap and the other sitting by his side. After our divorce, I continued the family plan to make sure that my children stayed immersed in sports. That meant a lot of sacrifices for me. I loved working. I loved the business world. Some things had to give, even if it meant giving up having an active social life. Sacrificing doesn't mean that your life comes to an end. It just means that you must give up some things for a certain period. Sacrifice is only for a period of time. It's temporary, not permanent. The rewards of sacrifice supersede the pain of the sacrifices you make. Today, when I look back, I regret none of the sacrifices that I made. The rewards have been plentiful and longstanding.

What do I mean when I say that the search for you can be long-standing? Essentially, I'm suggesting that in some facet of your life, someone can be searching for you for years. I have former co-workers or employees find me on Linked-In for job referrals, professional advice, or just to say hello. The search doesn't always have to be for professional reasons; the search can be romantically driven. Someone whose life you've impacted in a significant way might be looking for you. And thanks to modern technology, the search for long lost loved ones doesn't have to involve the expensive services of a private investigator. With a few clicks, you can locate people with whom you've had no contact with since childhood. It is true, love can come searching for you and find you when you least expect it.

If someone said the name Lawrence, it wouldn't have garnered any emotion from me. Thirty years had gone by, and I had long forgotten about the relationship I had with a young fella named Lawrence. Lawrence, on the other hand, hadn't forgotten about me, LaSonjia Fisher. Fisher is my maiden name. And even with advanced technology, Facebook, Instagram, Twitter, LinkedIn, and the like, he could not find LaSonjia Fisher anywhere. That's because I was no longer LaSonjia Fisher. Ever since I'd gotten married, which was in my twenties, I had used my married name, Jack. As fate would have it, Lawrence met someone who was mutual friends with a player's father on my son's NFL Football team. It was during a general conversation that the name "LaSonjia" came up. Here's how I was told it all unfolded.

"How is that new player on your son's team doing? Myles Jack, he is one of my favorite players." Lawrence said to the acquaintance.

"He is doing great, did you see those tackles in that last game?" said the player's father. "Also, I talked with his mom LaSonjia, she is so very happy about his plays. We see her at the games with family."

"What's her name?" said Lawrence

"LaSonjia." Said the player's father.

"That's a unique name," Lawrence said, do you know where she's from?"

"I believe from the Chicago area," said the player's father, "Why, do you know her?"

"Wow, that is such a consequence, It's not just her name that's unique. I've been looking for a LaSonjia Fisher. I've never met a woman that was so structured, ambitious, and driven as she was."

Is her last name Jack or Fisher?"

"It is LaSonjia Jack," said the player's father

"You said she is married, right?"

"No, she is not married that I know of,"

"I am going to do some research on this. I could not get her out of my mind. I can't explain it. It was something about LaSonjia that just made her stand out, even after all these years," Lawrence said.

"Well, do you want me to call her and see if this is the same person? Said the player's father.

"Yes, it's worth a try! She will know me as 'LO,' played college basketball, and from New Orleans. Let me know once you call her and I'll give you some clues to give to her. If this is her, ask her if I can get her number. I just can't believe this, after almost 30 years, this could be LaSonjia Fisher!"

And before it was all said and done, a few days later I received a phone call from the player's father. I happened to be in an airport getting ready to board a flight, I had about 20 minutes I could talk.

"Hi LaSonjia," said the player's dad. "I have someone who thinks they may know you."

My response was, "Yeah, many people think they know me, what you got?"

"Well, he said to say these three clues to you, and you should say his name."

I said, "Ok I'm about to board a flight so give me the clues."

He then said, "He played basketball, from New Orleans, knows your mom, sister, and brother and he is from New Orleans."

I thought for a moment and then I froze. I knew who it was. It was "LO."

I was taking a long time to respond so the player's dad said, "I told him he doesn't know you."

"No, I said, I know exactly who that is. How do you know him? His name is Lawrence."

Well guess what he said? "Lawrence has been looking for you,"

"Lawrence, wow a blast from the past!" I said, shocked.
"Yes, and he gave me his number to give to you." I think time stood still for about a good thirty seconds. I wrote his number down, but it took me several days to build up the nerve to call him.

You see, Lawrence and I had a fun-filled romance during the summer of 1988, which was more than thirty years previously. It was late 2019, more than thirty-one years later. I still had emotional scars from the divorce, and learning that someone had been searching for me for more than three decades was a bit intimidating. I was no longer that nineteen-year-old carefree young girl. I was a grown woman who was walking around with residue from past relationships.

It took some convincing from my best friends, for me to finally pick up the phone and call Lawrence.
"Do you know how long I've been looking for you?" was one of the first things that came out of Lawrence's mouth.

"I heard," I said, basking in the compliment for that split second.

"No, seriously, LaSonjia. There was something about you that set my soul on fire way back then. I know we were young, but I couldn't get you out of my system. You wouldn't go away, no matter how hard I tried to make you."

I thought that we'd enjoy that three-hour-long conversation and revert back to our own lives. But it didn't quite happen that way. Before the conversation ended, Lawrence popped the question —"I need to see you. When can I see you?"

I wiped the pebbles of sweat from my forehead. This was serious. See me? He wants to see me? "Ahh ... my schedule is a little crazy, so I'll look at my calendar and get back to you in a few days," I said. I was so caught off guard. It had been a long time since a man had been so direct and insistent on wanting to see me.

"Okay," Lawrence said. I could sense the disappointment in his voice, but I didn't want to seem thirsty, so I played it safe making the excuse of having to check my calendar.

To thine own self be true.

Over the next three days, I had candid conversations with myself. I had to ask myself why I was reluctant to visit a man that treated me like royalty when I was nineteen. A man who adored me and cherished the ground I walked on. And then, I had to ask myself whether I was being true to my own self, as Shakespeare had directed. I have a saying, which is, "I don't do baby steps."

I had to ask myself whether I was honoring my own word and declaration. If it was business related, I wouldn't have hesitated to check my calendar and make appropriate travel arrangements.

After three days, I finally called Lawrence back and agreed to meet him in Dallas, Texas. But the schedules did not work out so he asked me to come to a basketball tournament that his team was playing during Mother's Day weekend. I agreed, what did I have to lose?

Our planes would arrive about 30 minutes apart, and I would arrive early. I was awaiting him and his basketball team near the baggage claim area.

I was nervous until the moment our eyes met. There he was in the flesh, Lawrence, my 1988 love interest. I felt as though I was that fearless nineteen-year-old again. I was daring and unafraid. I knew I could rebound from pain.

"You look absolutely beautiful," Lawrence said, looking me over from head to toe. "I've been searching for you for thirty years! I was beginning to think that I would never see you again."

After thirty years, our lives were no longer simple. We'd both been married and divorced. We both had children. But it was like we had made an unspoken agreement to enjoy where we were and who we had become. For the next couple of days after I returned home, that's exactly what we did. I only stayed one day with Lawrence and flew back home for Mother's Day, to be with my boys. It was good to see an old acquaintance and he was still very funny, just like when I knew him 30 years before.

During my visit to see him coach his team I realized that something wasn't quite right with Lawrence … health-wise. His breathing seemed a little labored.

"Can you do me a favor?" I asked Lawrence.

"Anything for you, my love," Lawrence shot back.

"Can you promise me that you will do it?"

"Anything for you!"

"I need you to make an appointment with your doctor. Get a checkup. You know, make sure everything is okay."

Lawrence agreed. He told me he needed to tell me something very important but not right now. Lawrence promised to get a checkup that week.

"So, what did they say?" I asked later that week on the phone.

"Blockage. The doctors said I have a blockage in the arteries leading to my heart. But it's something they can fix." I had a pacemaker put in my heart years ago and now it's time to replace it.

"Fix? How?" I asked, looking for him to provide details. He joked it off by saying it was a simple procedure and he would be in the hospital the next day to have the surgery. So that night we talked on the phone in a three-way call with another one of his friends I had also known 30 years earlier.

He also told me that Lawrence has been talking about me for years and could not believe that I was Myles Jack's mom, a player that he tracked from his college to pro football career.

I received one more call from Lawrence before the night of his surgery.

"I said, hey why are calling you must rest before your surgery!"

He said, "I know but I wanted to tell you something."

I said, "Ok."

"I want to thank you for coming to see me last week. That meant the world to me. I know that you are busy with your own life, but you are the LaSonjia that I remembered, and I am very proud of you. I see your Facebook and Instagram and you are even more than I imagined. You are so smart and that is just how I remembered."

I said no problem, that is what friends do. And We said good night

The next morning, Lawrence had bi-pass surgery. He called me on FaceTime after the procedure, joking and laughing. He said he would call me back in an hour. It was a warm, pleasant conversation. Light. Joyful. Sweet. Within 2 hours, I would receive a call telling me that Lawrence passed away. To say I was devastated is a grave understatement.

I felt myself drifting into some type of depression in September 2021. I often wondered why God allowed Lawrence to come back into my life. In fact, if I am going to be truthful, I was mad at the situation, and he was so very happy to see me. We were just catching back up on old times.

Your healing is searching for you.

Prior to reuniting with Lawrence, I was still carrying around some emotional scars inflicted because of events that happened during my life, as well as scars from some of the not-so-good relationships I'd gotten involved in over the course of my life. For every insult I endured from a past relationship, Lawrence recited a poem of love. For every name I was called by my haters in high school, Lawrence had some great positive things to tell me. For all the teasing and bullying I endured for being poor and not being able to be a "normal" teenager, Lawrence told me how much he admired me. How much my being different set me apart.

To hear this from a person outside of the business world, meant the world to me.

God knew why I needed Lawrence in my life at that precise moment in my life. You see, my healing had been searching for me. And my healing was attached to Lawrence. He had a way of making me feel extra special and he told many stories that I didn't even remember when were young. How I was a planner and told him how I was going to have a great life. In fact, he told me that because of that conversation, he decided to get his own situation in order. When I met Lawrence, I didn't know he was a highly recruited basketball player who was going through a difficult time because his mom had just recently passed away. His sister had sent him to Chicago to clear his head when he met me. He said I brought him a new perspective on life and no other women had the same impact.

I'm still healing from Lawrence's sudden passing. Although the time was short, our interaction was kind ... enjoyable ... uplifting ... and fulfilling. It will be cherished forever.

Thank you, Lawrence. Thank you for following your heart. In it, you helped preserve mine. I now have a greater capacity to love.

Chapter 10 Exercises

Have you ever experienced a situation where someone was looking for you, whether it was for a professional reason or some other reason? If so, why do you think that person was searching for you? What about you made them look for you?

How do you think you can harness the skill or ability mentioned above to help your reach your goals?

Do you think that you have positioned your name to be mentioned in different circles outside of your presence? Why or why not?

Have you ever experienced a "Lawrence situation?" In other words, has anyone ever come into your life for a short period of time but left you with an experience of a lifetime? Share this experience.

What was your takeaway or takeaways from the experience? In other words, what did you learn? How did you grow?

Is there something in your life that you feel you need to heal from? Provide details.

Do you know what it would take to receive healing from what you've listed in Question 7?

CHAPTER 11
CHECKPOINTS

Think about the last time you were headed to a special event, to meet someone for lunch or dinner, or even en route home after a long day at work. The last thing you wanted to do was find yourself caught up in a law enforcement checkpoint. They stop you unexpectedly, and oftentimes, you don't see them before it's too late. Most often, too late simply means you can't make a U-turn to avoid them. Even if your papers are straight, your car is properly registered and insured, your license is valid- you'd still prefer to not get caught up in a checkpoint.

Fortunately, however, checkpoints, although they can be an inconvenience to us, serve a good purpose. Checkpoints are targeted to find impaired drivers, taking them off the road before tragedy can strike. Studies show that law enforcement checks are associated with a reduction in the number of alcohol-related crashes. This finding has a direct impact on the number of vehicular fatalities. Next, law enforcement checkpoints are geared to find illegal drivers (those who do not have a license to drive), or illegal activity.

Interestingly, however, there is a checkpoint strategy; checkpoints are not conducted randomly. During a checkpoint, law enforcement officers may stop every car or use a specific pattern, such as every third or fifth car, to ensure fairness and efficiency. Checkpoints are planned at the state and regional levels. In fact, some cities and towns are known to regularly conduct these checks.

During a checkpoint law enforcement officers will typically ask the driver for their license, registration, and proof of insurance. They may also ask the driver a few questions, such as where they are coming from and where they are going. If the officer suspects that the driver may be impaired, they may conduct a field sobriety test, which often involves asking the driver to perform certain physical and cognitive tasks such as standing on one leg or reciting the alphabet. If the driver fails the test or exhibits other signs of impairment, they may be arrested for DUI (driving under the influence). In this case, the checkpoint is effective and has served its purpose.

You might ask, "What does a law enforcement checkpoint have to do with me or my life?" Well, I'm glad you asked. Checkpoints are critical in our lives as they help us assess our progress, make adjustments, and set new goals- just to name a few things. During this chapter, I need you to conduct yourself as the Governor of your life's journey. You are working with your administration to set up these checkpoints in your state (In other words your LIFE). Just as checkpoints are important in physical journeys, they are also important in the journey of life.

Checkpoints in our lives can be defined as moments or events that represent a significant milestone or turning point in our personal or professional journey. These checkpoints can take many forms, such as a graduation, a job promotion, a marriage, the birth of a child, or even a personal achievement like running a marathon. These moments often mark a transition from one phase of life to another, and they can have a profound impact on our future trajectory. You can have a goal and achieve that goal - and keep running right past the goal. In the end, you will have robbed yourself out of celebrating the achievement and any expected OUTCOMES. To provide greater context, outcomes are the expectations for what our goals will establish. In other words, what benefit will the achieved goal bring?

We often fail to think about goal outcomes, let alone evaluate them. I'll share my experience on evaluating goal outcomes.

Earlier in my career, I was assigned to work on the iPhone launch at AT&T. It was in the mid-2000s. During this time, the iPhone rollout was similar to today's AI (artificial intelligence) rollout to the public. The iPhone was a gamechanger in the telecommunications industry. I worked tirelessly with cross-functional teams on the product launch. Finally, after months of hard work, the iPhone product launch was a success on January 9th, 2007. But what happened immediately afterward was an immediate eyeopener and caused me to identify the blind spots in my goal settings.

Within weeks of the successful product launch, many of my colleagues were being promoted. Some of them were even recruited by other competitor companies, such as Verizon, Sprint, and T-Mobile. Yet, there I was, still in the same role and position. I wasn't immediately promoted. And while I was genuinely happy for my colleagues, I had to take a look at myself. I had to have a serious come-to-Jesus moment and ask myself this question: "Why have you not been promoted, LaSonjia?"

That's when it dawned on me—I didn't have any expected outcomes assigned to the product launch whereas my colleagues did. For them, the iPhone rollout was a launching pad to a promotion. While the goal was to be a part of a successful product launch, the outcome was a new role or promotion.

I needed to conduct a checkpoint to set new goals, prioritize some goals, set benchmarks, change my mindset, and establish outcomes for every new goal I set. As painful as the experience was, I learned from it. All was not lost, however, because after conducting the checkpoint, I positioned myself for a new promotion. I updated my resume, including the highlights of the most recent iPhone product launch. I applied for new roles. Before long, I landed a new job, one offering a title upgrade, more money, perks, and of course, more responsibilities. My new role had more responsibilities as I was named the Regional Director of Business to Business (B2B) Sales for T-Mobile that spans across 7 states. In the end, I learned a valuable lesson from a painful experience.

When was the last time you conducted a checkpoint in your life? Better yet, have you ever conducted a life checkpoint? Have you established outcomes for your goals? In other words, ask yourself, "What do I want to get out of meeting this goal?" Do you want recognition? Promotion? More clients? Business expansion? Less Stress? New relationship? Better health? More finances?

You must assign outcomes to your goals and evaluate whether the expectations are met. This will be one transformation in your life, but you will have many. The business term is called "program evaluation." A program evaluation is essentially a checkpoint. As previously stated, checkpoints are critical. Below is a brief list of the benefits of conducting a life and goal checkpoint.

- **Set goals.**

Checkpoints are critical in setting goals for ourselves. Without checkpoints, we might not be aware of where we stand in relation to our objectives. When we set goals, we need to define what success means to us, what we want to achieve, and what steps we need to take to get there. Checkpoints help us break down our goals into smaller, more manageable tasks, which we can evaluate regularly to ensure we are on track. This helps us stay focused and motivated, and it also helps us to adjust our goals if necessary.

- **Prioritize.**

Checkpoints help us to prioritize our goals and identify which goals are most important to us. Is your work life chaotic? Is your desk or office space a mess? Is your garage a mess? Do you feel that you are all over the place? Well, it's time to get things in order by importance. It is essential to focus on our most significant objectives to achieve our desired results. Checkpoints help us to evaluate the importance of our goals and to make sure we are focusing on what matters most.

- **Measure Progress.**

Checkpoints are important in measuring progress towards our goals. They help us to monitor our progress and to identify areas where we need to improve. Are you moving the needle ? Is your new change happening? Think of it as a measuring stick, are you in the same place or have you moved down the lines of accomplishing your tasks? By measuring our progress regularly, we can identify what is working and what is not working and make changes as necessary. You have to keep things progressing even if it is a snail's pace, you must reach your goals. Make rapid changes if needed, don't wait. Adjust whatever is in the way of accomplishing your dreams.

- **Stay Accountable.**

Checkpoints help us to stay accountable to ourselves and to others. Are you working with an accountability partner or partners? This is the person/s that you selected earlier in your progress to ensure that you follow through on achieving your goals. With your new business do you have employees that you are now responsible for? Are you holding yourself accountable for ensuring that you are moving the business along? It is so valuable to ensure that we are committing to a plan, and we are making ourselves accountable for achieving our goals. When we have accountability, we are more likely to complete tasks associated with our goals. In the end, we are more likely to achieve the goals we have set.

- **Stay on Track.**

Checkpoints are important in helping us to stay on track towards our goals. Life can be busy, and distractions can be common. Are you writing down your tasks? Is your calendar full of things that you need to get completed? Whether it is important meetings, additional training, travel, or developing a new product or service, make sure you have dates and deadlines next to these items. When we set checkpoints, we are creating a structure that can help us stay on track, even when life gets busy. Checkpoints help us to prioritize our goals and ensure we are making progress towards achieving them.

- **Make Adjustments.**

Checkpoints help us to make adjustments when necessary. As we progress toward our goals, we may encounter challenges or obstacles that require us to adjust our plans. This is one of the hardest areas to embrace, because most people don't want to stop in order to make changes, even when things may not be going as planned.

It's hard to change your resources, a marketing plan or even the people who you are working with, because that was your original plan. We all sometimes get locked into our expectations of how things are going to happen. We all do better when we know better- and to be successful in directing our future we must make those bold moves early in our process. Checkpoints help us to recognize when changes are needed and to make them in a timely manner. By making adjustments, we can ensure we are on track to achieve our objectives.

Reflect. Checkpoints offer an opportunity to reflect on what we have achieved so far and what we need to do differently to achieve our goals.

- **Reflection.**

Reflection is crucial in our personal growth and development. It helps us to recognize our strengths and weaknesses and identify areas where we need to improve. In order to reflect, I need you to take a moment. Sit somewhere very quietly and think about the future.

What does that look like for you? Imagine you have met your goals, what does it feel like? Savor that feeling. That is where you're trying to go. Imagine all of your goals are met and you are excelling beyond measure.

This exercise can help us to learn and grow, and it can help us to apply what we have learned to future situations. By reflecting on our progress, we can also celebrate our achievements and take pride in our hard work.

- **Stay motivated.**

Checkpoints help us to stay motivated by providing a sense of accomplishment and progress. If you're starting to feel unmotivated, get with your accountability partners/s and explain to them how you are feeling. They are there to provide support and remind you of the accomplishments that you have already completed. Go back in your mind and remember why you started this journey in the first place. You can do this! You can get this new endeavor off and running. You are so very capable to attain this success. Believe in your own ability.

When we achieve our goals or make progress towards them, we feel a sense of satisfaction that motivates us to continue working towards our objectives.

- **Celebrate our achievements.**

Finally, checkpoints allow us to celebrate our achievements. When we reach a significant milestone, we can take the time to acknowledge our hard work and dedication and celebrate our success with family and friends. REWARD yourself. These rewards don't need to be necessarily monetary. I tend to put on a great song and dance around the room when I have completed some of my biggest tasks! Pat yourself on the back. This is good energy. I like to go get a new nail color on my nails, or take a friend out to lunch and celebrate your accomplishments. This celebration can be a source of joy and inspiration, motivating us to continue striving for success in the future.

It may be the actual delivery of your new product, or you are in various interviews for a new position, or you just completed a new painting that you will sell, or just created your final prototype of your new product... whatever the goal looked like, you made it! Celebrate Celebrate Celebrate!!!

You are on your way and your plans are working! One of the most significant benefits of checkpoints is that they help us evaluate our progress. By reflecting on our achievements and setbacks, we can gain insight into our strengths and weaknesses and identify areas where we need to improve. This self-reflection allows us to set new goals and develop strategies to achieve them.

Now that you know the benefit of conducting a checkpoint, you need to know HOW to do it in a useful way. You need a strategy. Below, I've outlined a basic strategy you can follow to conduct your own checkpoints.

Performing a Life Checkpoint Strategy

- **Define Objectives.**

Clearly identify the areas of your life that you want to assess and improve. This could include career, relationships, health, personal growth, new business, creating a new product or service, upgrading your finances, or any area of your life where you are determined to make a difference. Set specific goals and objectives for each area.

- **Evaluate Current State.**

Take a comprehensive look at your current situation in each area. Assess your strengths, weaknesses, opportunities, and threats. Most importantly, how is your mental and psychological state? You may need to address your mental health, even though we often overlook this area. Our mind and body is one, so we must have a plan to assist in this area if needed. Analyze what is working well and what needs improvement.

- **Gather Information.**

Collect relevant data and information related to your objectives. This can include self-reflection, feedback from others, performance metrics, financial records, and any other pertinent sources. Find an expert in the field that you are trying to find success in. Don't reinvent the wheel, you can gain important lessons quickly, and save time, by finding an expert to help you in this process.

- **Reflect and Assess.**

Take the time to reflect on your findings. Assess the overall alignment of your current state with your desired objectives. Identify areas where you excel and areas that require attention or change. Find reflection techniques that inspire you to reflect often. I recommend the following: Breathing exercises to help relax in tense or stressful situations. Closing your eyes and meditating is very good. Going to an exercise or yoga class may be helpful for your mind and body. Watching a meditation video on YouTube or taking a long, thoughtful walk are both calming for some people. Are you listening to positive things? Perhaps a favorite motivational speaker to get you energized and focused on the plan. What you put into your mind directly reflects what you put out into the universe. Know that you will grow during this process. You will be better in every way.

- **Set Priorities.**

Prioritize the areas that require the most immediate attention or improvement. Determine which aspects will have the greatest impact on your overall well-being and success. Get rid of the noise. Don't complete tasks that will not take you to where you need to go. Prioritize often, things will shift and that is OK. That is supposed to happen as you travel on your journey.

- **Develop Action Plans.**

Create actionable steps to address each priority area. Set specific and measurable goals, outline strategies, and define milestones. Break down large goals into smaller, manageable tasks. Review these plans weekly.

- **Implement Changes.**

Start fulfilling your action plans. NO procrastination. Let's get going with these efforts. Dedicate time to making positive changes in your prioritized areas. Seek support, resources, and guidance as needed. Make this area a habit, a regular part of your process.

- **Monitor and Adjust.**

Regularly review your progress and make necessary adjustments along the way. Stay adaptable and flexible as circumstances may change. Celebrate successes and learn from setbacks.

- **Seek Support and Accountability.**

Consider involving a mentor, coach, or trusted friend who can provide guidance, support, and hold you accountable for your actions and progress. USE them often, it will help you stay focused and keep you motivated.

- **Review and Repeat.**

Periodically perform life checkpoints to reassess your objectives, progress, and set new goals. Continually strive for personal growth, mental strength, and improvement. Life is so very wonderful, so take control of it!

Remember, a life checkpoint is an ongoing process that requires commitment and dedication. By regularly assessing and adjusting your life's direction, you can make meaningful progress towards your goals and live a more fulfilling and purposeful life.

If you don't remember anything else from this chapter, the key takeaway is that checkpoints in our lives are essential for personal growth, professional development, and overall well-being. They allow us to evaluate our progress, celebrate our achievements, set new goals, gain direction or even change direction and purpose. You will have many successes along the way. Get ready to embrace them all.

Chapter 11 Exercises

The questions below are geared to help you develop a concrete checkpoint strategy. They are instructed to help stimulate self-reflection, provide insights into areas of improvement, and assist in creating a clear roadmap for personal growth and development.

What areas of your life would you like to assess and evaluate during this life checkpoint?

How would you define success or fulfillment in each of those areas?

What specific goals or objectives do you have for each area of your life?

How do you currently measure progress or success in those areas? Are you reflecting on what is working and what is not?

What are the biggest challenges or obstacles you face in achieving your desired outcomes? What do you need to stop doing immediately?

What resources or support systems do you currently have in place to help you in your journey? Who are your accountability partners? Who are your experts?

How do you handle setbacks or failures in pursuing your goals? Give an example.

Are there any patterns or habits that you feel are holding you back from reaching your full potential? List them here.

How do you prioritize your time and energy among different areas of your life?

How will you hold yourself accountable for implementing the necessary changes identified during this life checkpoint?

Chapter 12
Looking Out for #1 - Every day is Christmas!

Your life isn't just about striving for success without taking the time to pause, reflect, and celebrate your achievements. Celebrating your accomplishments and embracing the things you enjoy in life are essential for your overall well-being and happiness.

In the relentless pursuit of success, it is easy to become overwhelmed and burned out. Taking the time to celebrate your achievements and enjoy life helps you sustain motivation and combat burnout.

Celebration acts as a powerful motivator, providing a much-needed boost of energy and inspiration to continue working towards your goals. Let's look at the reasons why it's crucial to celebrate achievements. As you move through your day-to-day priorities, it should feel like it's Christmas. Your gift can vary every day. From a smile by a passing neighbor, a free cup of coffee, words of wisdom from an unknown source, or someone just doing something out of the ordinary for you would be considered a gift.

It can even be you treating yourself to the things, learning, and experiences that make you happy. It could be a special gift that comes your way directly or indirectly. If you ask my close friends, they will hear me say, "It's Christmas again today!" and I always have special gifts that I have received during my day.

How do you create a world where it's Christmas every day? Well, I'm glad you asked!

- **Acknowledge Progress.**

When we celebrate our achievements, big or small, we acknowledge our progress and give ourselves a well-deserved pat on the back. There are inherent benefits to celebrating our successes. It helps to boost our self-esteem, reinforcing the belief in our capabilities and fostering a positive self-image. By recognizing our achievements, we gain confidence, motivation, and a sense of fulfillment that propels us forward. Right now, take a moment and pat yourself on the back for all the tasks you have completed or where you have gained momentum towards your goals.

- **Cultivate Positive Mindset and Foster Gratitude.**

Celebrating our achievements and indulging in activities we enjoy helps cultivate a positive mindset and fosters gratitude. When we acknowledge and celebrate our successes, we shift our focus from what we lack to what we have accomplished. This positive perspective allows us to appreciate the journey and the blessings in our lives. By embracing gratitude, we invite more joy and positivity into our everyday experiences. The glass is always full in my mind, never half empty as others may see it.

- **Strengthening Relationships and Building Connections.**

Celebrating our achievements and embracing the things we enjoy in life not only benefit us individually but also strengthen our relationships and build connections with others. Sharing our successes and celebrations with loved ones creates a sense of community and fosters deeper connections. By involving others in our joyous moments, we create memories and forge bonds that can last a lifetime.

- **Enhancing Overall Well-being and Life Satisfaction.**

Taking the time to celebrate our achievements and prioritize activities that bring us joy enhances our overall well-being and life satisfaction. When we balance our pursuit of success with moments of celebration and enjoyment, we create a harmonious and fulfilling lifestyle. By nurturing our physical, mental, and emotional well-being through celebration, we experience greater happiness, reduced stress, and improved overall quality of life, which leads us to the pathway of discovering true joy.

What is joy? Joy is a deep sense of happiness, contentment, and fulfillment. It is an emotion that goes beyond temporary pleasure and reflects a state of well-being and inner peace. Joy is often associated with a sense of gratitude, appreciation, and a profound connection to oneself, others, or the world around us.

There's one great misconception about joy. Many people think that joy is about luxury living and spending, and this can be the furthest thing from the truth. True joy often lies in the SIMPLE pleasures of life. Despite what advertisements show us, there are a plethora of pathways leading to the discovery of joy.

I'll share with you a personal experience of mine. When I was younger, I thought I had to do it all without sufficient rest and minimal time for a social life, all while fulfilling the roles of mom, daughter, sister, and corporate manager.

I can distinctly remember lying in bed one Saturday morning reflecting on my life and the world around me. My sons were doing well in school and sports, I was helping my family complete various tasks, I made sure to hit all the targets and deadlines on my job, making sure my team performed well and the team members were well positioned for success and promotion, and I'd even gone the extra mile for some of my associates and friends.

While I had a hand in the happiness and successes of those around me, I wasn't really that happy. In fact, I felt empty and sort of lost. Then it dawned me—I had not looked out for number one … me. I had poured into everybody else's life but had neglected to attend to my own needs. That's when I made up my mind that I was no longer going to neglect my own needs. I was no longer going to just accept congratulatory remarks, emails, or even plaques for my accomplishments at work. I was going to celebrate the academic and sports achievements of my son's right along with them. And then, I was going to celebrate the achievement of others, especially the achievements of those close to me in which I played some part.

LaSonjia was going to look out for #1. "Every day is Christmas." Whether you believe in holidays or not, it is a metaphor I use to mean that you should enjoy life every day, and it should bring you gifts. It's important to keep an eye out for them. Life's little gifts are easy to take for granted.

Those gifts could include new learning, interacting with new people, laughter and joy, a motivating message that you heard, or the clerk at your department store found the extra discount coupon to help you out with your purchase.

In that moment of introspection, the first thing I did was ... you guessed it—grabbed a pen and paper and started writing. I jotted down the things I used to do but felt I no longer had the time to do.

Next, I jotted down some of my aspirational goals. I wrote down all the things I wanted to do but never made the time for. When I finished, I had a list of about 50 things. To my surprise, the vast majority of the things on my list could've been done without breaking the bank.

As I mentioned earlier, celebrating yourself and finding joy are not synonymous with costly expenses. A trip to the park or nearby beach to enjoy nature, reading a great book, or listening to soothing music cost nothing more than packing a healthy lunch, putting a little gas in the tank, and taking the drive to the venue.

What you'll get in return for time and money spent is much more than you invested. In just a couple of hours, you can rejuvenate your mind, body, spirit, and soul. For example, one day it seemed to be Christmas all day: I had my luggage damaged during a flight with my favorite airline, Delta. The baggage attendant was very helpful with me filling out a claim form. I took my luggage to get fixed from one of my favorite places, Tumi luggage. They told me that they could not fix it but offered me a refund to purchase another new piece of luggage.

Then when I told Delta, they also provided me with a refundable amount which allowed me to upgrade all of my luggage and I would need that luggage as I have just been informed that I made the Delta Million Miler status.

You may call this luck, but I call it Christmas. As I continue to place positive seeds in the universe, I receive special gifts everyday, and I look for them.

If you can recall, you'll remember that my father was responsible for me developing a love of all kinds of music and dance. When I was lying in bed that Saturday morning, I realized that I hadn't even enjoyed a live concert in quite some time. While listening to music is one thing, going to a live concert is altogether something different. Live music offers a different experience. For one, the energy at a live concert is high and engaging. The intensity of the musical performance itself can be so electrifying that it causes you to forget about your problems and just live right there in the moment.

That's what we often forget to do—live in the moment. When we overlook "the moment" and focus on our future birthday, planning Christmas for the family, or planning a vacation; it robs us of the joy and the excitement that the present moment offers.

Look at it this way, tomorrow doesn't exist. It's just a conceptual construct. It's not tangible or visible. We have no power over tomorrow, next week, next month, or next year. We only have power over what we can do today. And thinking of it this way can empower you. Ask yourself, what can you do today that can change your tomorrow? Are you willing to live the rest of your life empty and feeling powerless? What are you doing to make everyday Christmas? Are you just existing or putting forth effort to enjoy the world that we live in? Are you being your best self?

I often talk to people about the joy that they are creating in their lives. For example, I mentored a young businessman in his 20s. He was just starting a new career path at a new company. He was not very confident about his performance. He had a small team and he spent time trying to perfect his leadership skills. In order to help, I wanted to understand what communication techniques he used with his team.

What we uncovered was that he did not lead his team with positivity and joy. Due to his lack of team leadership and experience, he did not exhibit happiness. In fact, he dreaded coming in to work each day. He didn't realize that he was projecting that unhappiness with his team. He was creating a culture of disconnect with his team. I advised him to find a class to help him learn team building, and use it to enhance the connectedness of his team.

During my recent check-in with him he was doing much better. His team was working as one unit. By showing positivity and communicating effectively with his team, he improved his entire work culture.

He had to first realize that he had an issue within himself and then look at each person on his team and find ways to improve the energy with that person. Now every day can be Christmas with his team. He's providing feedback instantly and giving them tools to enhance their expectations of the team.

Feedback is free and listening to his team is also free. He can now focus on removing obstacles and infusing a positive work environment. He had some personal issues that were not good, and he had to find ways to resolve them. With some outside counseling, he was able to get back on track. That is also a Christmas present. The gift of having a very good personal life will also bleed into your business life. Those two will always meet up at some point so you must pay attention to both areas.

Feeling fulfilled is as simple as discovering pathways to joy. Being thankful and grateful in the present moment can help you appreciate the simple pleasures in life. Paying attention to the small moments of happiness, practicing gratitude for what you have, and focusing on the present can all bring a profound sense of joy.

- **Pursue Meaningful Relationships.**

Building and nurturing meaningful connections with others can contribute to joy. Engaging in acts of kindness, showing empathy, and fostering genuine relationships can create a sense of joy and fulfillment that comes from shared experiences and support. Are the individuals that you spend time with positive, fun, and loving?

- **Engage in Activities that Bring Joy.**

Identify activities, hobbies, or pursuits that bring you joy and make them a regular part of your life. This could include anything from creative endeavors, sports, spending time in nature, or engaging in acts of service. Prioritize activities that genuinely resonate with you and bring you a sense of joy and purpose. Is there something that you wanted to do, but just for some reason have not?

- **Embrace Mindset Shifts.**

Adopting a positive mindset and focusing on the good aspects of life can help cultivate joy. Letting go of negative thoughts, practicing self-compassion, and embracing optimism can create a more joyful outlook on life. Start the morning with a positive motivation and end the day the same way. I found some motivational rocks with positive affirmations that I can look at each day. They say Blessed, Happiness and Wealth.

- **Embrace the Journey.**

Joy can be found in the process rather than solely focusing on outcomes. Embrace the journey of personal growth, learning, and overcoming challenges. Finding joy in the pursuit of your goals and celebrating small victories along the way can bring immense joy and satisfaction. Remember that the journey towards embracing the things you love is ongoing, and it requires commitment, flexibility, and self-compassion. Take the first step today, and let the joy of travel, socializing, hobbies, language learning, and creative pursuits enrich your life in meaningful ways. Embrace the things that light up your soul and create a life that truly reflects your passions and values.

- **Look Out For Number One.**

Looking out for number one is mandatory if you intend to live a fulfilling and well-rounded life. In other words, making time for the things you enjoy is not a luxury but a necessity. Author Robert J. Ringer explains the notion perfectly in his book, "Looking Out for Number One."

"Looking Out for Number One" is a thought-provoking and introspective book that delves into the concept of self-interest and advocates for individuals to prioritize their own well-being and success to lead an empowered life. The author challenges conventional wisdom and societal expectations that often encourage selflessness and sacrifice at the expense of personal growth and happiness. He argues that embracing self-interest is not synonymous with selfishness, but rather a necessary step towards achieving personal fulfillment and contributing positively to the world. Throughout the book, the author explores various aspects of self-interest, including setting boundaries, making choices aligned with personal values, and understanding the importance of self-preservation. I believe that if you don't take care of yourself, you cannot fully take care of others.

Ringer draws on personal anecdotes, real-life examples, and philosophical insights to illustrate his points and encourage readers to question the status quo. He addresses common fears and misconceptions associated with self-interest, challenging readers to reevaluate their beliefs and consider the benefits of looking out for oneself without compromising the well-being of others. The author does not neglect to emphasize the benefits of looking out for number one as well as the drawbacks of not looking out for one's own interests. An abbreviated list of pros and cons is described below.

- **Personal Growth and Fulfillment.**

Prioritizing self-care allows us to nurture our own growth and fulfillment. By focusing on our needs, desires, and goals, we can invest in personal development, explore our passions, and achieve a sense of self-actualization.

- **Improved Physical and Mental Health.**

Taking care of ourselves physically and mentally is crucial for overall well-being. When we prioritize self-care, we can maintain good health, manage stress levels, and prevent burnout. This, in turn, enables us to show up as our best selves in various aspects of life.

- **Enhanced Relationships.**

By attending to our own needs, we can foster healthier relationships with others. When we feel fulfilled and balanced, we have more to give and can engage in meaningful connections from a place of abundance rather than depletion.

- **Increased Productivity and Success.**

Investing in self-care can boost productivity and drive success in other areas of life. When we prioritize our well-being, we replenish our energy, enhance focus, and increase our ability to perform at our best.

Those are some wonderful examples of what self care can do for you. But what if it's missing? What are the costs of failing to care for yourself first?

- **Physical and Mental Exhaustion.**

Neglecting self-care can lead to physical and mental exhaustion, compromising our overall health and well-being. Overextending ourselves for the sake of others can result in burnout, decreased productivity, and decreased satisfaction in our personal and professional lives. Right now, if this is how you are feeling, go seek help immediately. Communicate this to a friend or family member that will hold you accountable to seek some assistance. Sometimes we need a person who is on the outside to provide a sounding board. We need to release our thoughts that swirl in our minds so we can make it clear to focus on our projects and goals without all of the interference that clouds our minds.

- **Resentment and Lack of Boundaries.**

When we consistently prioritize others' needs at the expense of our own, we may develop feelings of resentment and frustration. Neglecting self-interest can erode boundaries, leading to a lack of self-respect and enabling others to take advantage of our generosity.

- **Hindered Personal Growth.**

Neglecting self-interest can hinder personal growth and limit our potential. By constantly prioritizing others, we may miss out on opportunities for self-discovery, learning, and pursuing our own passions and goals.

- **Strained Relationships.**

Neglecting self-interest can strain relationships as it creates an imbalance in giving and receiving. Constantly sacrificing our own needs can lead to a lack of authenticity and fulfillment in relationships, potentially causing resentment or dependency dynamics.

Remember, taking care of yourself is not selfish. It is a necessary foundation for living a joyful and meaningful life. By prioritizing self-care we can enhance our physical and mental well-being, nurture personal growth, foster healthier relationships, and achieve greater success. However, it's important to find a harmonious equilibrium between self-interest and selflessness, avoiding the pitfalls of neglecting one's own needs. By embracing the importance of self-care, we not only benefit ourselves but also become better equipped to contribute positively to the world around us.

Everyday can be Christmas for you!!!

Chapter 12 Exercises

The goal of this exercise is to help you explore and implement self-care practices based on the principles outlined in Robert J. Ringer's book, "Looking Out for Number One."

Sections 1-4 are targeted to help you explore, prioritize, and embrace the things you love, whether it's traveling, socializing with friends, pursuing hobbies, learning new skills, or indulging in creative pursuits. By implementing these strategies, you can create a more balanced and fulfilling life.

Section 1: Reflection and Self-Assessment

A. *Take some time to reflect on your current lifestyle and habits. Consider areas where you may be neglecting your own well-being or putting others' needs before your own. List them and try to identify the reason or reasons why you might be neglecting them (e.g., oversight, not wanting to be criticized, guilt, etc.).*

B. *Identify activities, hobbies, or practices that bring you joy, relaxation, and fulfillment. These could be things you used to enjoy or new activities you would like to explore.*

C. *Evaluate your boundaries and personal limits. Reflect on situations where you may need to assert yourself more effectively and set healthy boundaries.*

Section 2: Personalized Self-Care Plan

A. Create a list of self-care activities that align with your interests and needs. These can include physical, emotional, mental, and spiritual well-being practices.

B. Prioritize your self-care activities based on their importance to you and their potential impact on your overall well-being.

C. Establish a routine or schedule for incorporating these activities into your daily or weekly life. Consider setting aside dedicated time for self-care, even if it's just a few minutes each day.

Section 3: Implementing Self-Care Activities

A. Choose one self-care activity from your list and engage in it mindfully. Pay attention to how it makes you feel and the positive impact it has on your well-being. Describe the experience.

B. Experiment with different activities over time to find what works best for you. Remember that self-care is a personal journey, and what works for others may not necessarily work for you.

C. Reflect on any challenges or barriers that may arise in practicing self-care, and list them. Explore strategies to overcome these obstacles and find ways to make self-care a consistent part of your life.

Section 4: Regular Self-Reflection

A. Set aside time for regular self-reflection. Evaluate how well you are sticking to your self-care plan and whether any adjustments or modifications are needed. Write down what improvements you can make.

B. Check in with yourself emotionally and mentally. Assess your stress levels and emotional well-being and identify areas where additional self-care may be beneficial. List out the things that are stressful, and what additional self-care techniques might make a difference in those areas.

C. List things that have happened in your life in the last month that would fit into the "Every day is Christmas" experience.

Chapter 13
Giving Back & The Law of Return

What do I do now that I've worked long and hard, setting goals in place, creating a To-Do list, executed accordingly, and have now begun to reap the benefits and rewards?

Well, I'm glad you asked, because I am happy to tell you that now it's time to give back. It's time to mentor others. Sow into someone's business. Volunteer in your church and community. Pay for a college or continuing education course for someone that may need it. Give away what you no longer need or have use for. Pay for someone's registration to a professional conference. Do it without charge. Do not look for anything in return.

We will discuss the principle of the "Law of Return" later on in this chapter. For now, we will focus on giving, because the principle of giving is what turns the wheels of return.

Let's look at the concept of giving and why it's both necessary and relevant. The concept of giving back is deeply rooted in various religious traditions. There are many passages of Scripture that emphasize the moral obligation to share one's blessings with others. The principle of stewardship is central, highlighting that the resources individuals possess are ultimately gifts from a higher power, and thus, individuals are morally obligated to use these resources for the greater good. In other words, you are not to hoard your blessings. Now, this doesn't mean that you empty your bank account or give away any of your material possessions out of misunderstanding, guilt, or pressure. There are principles and laws set in place for a reason, and you can bet your life that when you adhere to them, you are faithfully rewarded, and when you don't, you receive penalties accordingly.

There are many ways that you can give back; giving back is not just associated with finances or what one can give without blinking an eye. We have millionaires all over the world and many of these people we will never hear about, not because the world is so large, but because many want to remain inconspicuous.

We live in a world where most people are centered around themselves and the riches they have stored up for themselves. I'm not suggesting that those who have accumulated a lot of wealth must become household names. What I am suggesting is that your name should be known by someone, even if that person is part of an organization (be it nonprofit or otherwise), because you have given back in some form. Perhaps you've lent your genius to help solve a problem, given money to for a noble cause, volunteered your time to sit with the elderly or disabled... Your greatness will always be tied to what you give and not what you have.

Some of the notable ways that people give are described below:

- **Philanthropy**

Throughout history numerous individuals and families have engaged in philanthropy, establishing foundations and donating significant sums to address social issues. Examples include the Rockefeller Foundation, the Gates Foundation, and the Chan Zuckerberg Initiative.

- **Social Justice Movements**

Various social justice movements, driven by moral imperatives, advocate for giving back to marginalized communities. Movements like the Civil Rights Movement and contemporary efforts for environmental justice highlight the importance of addressing systemic issues through collective action.

- **Corporate Social Responsibility (CSR)**

In the business world, the concept of CSR reflects a moral obligation for companies to contribute positively to society. Many successful companies integrate philanthropy, sustainability, and ethical business practices into their operations. You can always give back by joining or collaborating with these types of initiatives. Networking opportunities are endless. You are bound to get something in return for your time and efforts.

As you accumulate wealth or resources, there is a moral and ethical responsibility to give back to society. Acknowledging the interconnectedness of humanity and the privilege that comes with success encourages a commitment to social responsibility.

A profound principle of giving can be found in the Gospel of Luke 12:48 (NIV), where it states, "From everyone who has been given much, much will be demanded; and from the one who has been entrusted with much, much more will be asked."

Essentially, this means that if you are blessed to inherit or receive much, then much will be required of you. There is responsibility attached to every gift you have or blessing you receive. Being in a position to share your gifts, talents, and resources is one of the greatest experiences you could ever have.

The fruit of giving is boundless. Just take a look at some of the benefits and rewards that stem from giving:

- **Positive Impact on Mental Health**

Research suggests that acts of kindness and charitable giving can positively impact mental health. Engaging in altruistic behaviors is linked to increased levels of happiness, reduced stress, and a sense of purpose.

- **Economic Empowerment**

Economically, giving back can create opportunities for empowerment, particularly for marginalized or underserved communities. It aligns with ethical principles of economic justice and fairness, aiming to bridge economic disparities.

- **Spiritual Enrichment.**

Giving back enhances your spiritual development and is often viewed as a path to personal growth and enrichment.

- **Generational Wealth and Longevity.**

Giving back also involves considering the impact of your actions on future generations, including your own lineage. As previously discussed, as a futuristic thinker, you must think beyond the here and now. Like Harvard University, thinking ahead leads to long-term success. Just imagine your great-great-great grandchildren living off the fruits of your giving. You have the power to make it happen!

Acts of generosity and giving inspire others to do the same. Leading by example can create a ripple effect, encouraging a culture of kindness, empathy, and philanthropy within communities.

When it comes to giving, it's imperative that you practice what you preach. If you want to expand your reach, your track record must precede you.

Giving back is a principle that I've also taught my sons when they were young. Both Myles and Jahlen know the benefits and rewards of giving back—it not only empowers them but the world around them.

Here are a few achievements of my son Myles due to his efforts around giving back to his community. This makes me so proud. He understands the law of helping others and favors will continue to follow him.

- Winner of the Jacksonville Jaguars NFL Walter Payton Nominee Winner
- 2020 Jaguars Foundation Community Leadership MVP Award
- Jaguars Salute to Service Nominee (Jaguars Team & NFL

Nomination)
- Participated in the USO Tour (Jaguars Team & NFL Nomination)
- Scholarship for Edward Waters College Students
- Conducted a Back to School Bowling Bash Event for children (school supplies, candies and an afternoon of fun provided to the children)
- Donation to citizens in need – paid power bill
- Sponsored children with a Shop With A Jaguar experience during Christmas (each child received a bike, $100 gift card, dinner and a custom event t-shirt)
- Donation of gift cards (Publix & Academy Sports & Outdoors) for a westside Jacksonville Park, football team and cheerleading group. (Donation included Jaguars giveaway items and groceries)
- Participated in the NFL Mexico Visit (Jaguars Team & NFL Mexico Nomination)
- High School Visits to speak to students

Below is a partial list of the ways I have given back.
That coffee line is my favorite, I pay for the person's coffee behind me.

- I help many individuals that I do not know with their resumes, help to enhance it so that it is ready to be seen by a potential employer.
- Giving business advice to a new and upcoming business, how to market, build a brand, get meetings scheduled. How to move to the next level.
- Our Family Foundation provides scholarships each year to high school and college students

- Dollar General, it was a Saturday, and it was a long line, I went up to the cashier and said, "I'll take care of everyone's purchases, Today is Christmas." People were shocked but thanked me very much.
- The grocery store, helping some of our elders with their grocery purchases.
- Our family is focused on helping the military, we provide back to school backpacks and school supplies to the children as their mom or dad are deployed helping our nation.
- Prayer... I have stopped to pray with people and offer some motivational messages and provide details about my life that may help them on their journey.
- Mentorship is a big one, I have spent time with 100's of individuals providing structured and unstructured coaching on many topics both business and personal.
- In our family business we ensure that we focus on education and our youth, they are our future. Speaking to parents and family members about their children playing sports or ensuring that school is a focus, we will continue to help in this area.

The Law of Return

Giving back takes time, which sometimes we are very limited in. From my example above some of the givebacks can take money but helping others most of the time is a free effort. You just have to do it. If you have the gift of accounting, you can volunteer to be on the board of a non-profit, or if you sew very well you can help someone make costumes for a children's play, or you can create things to give as unexpected gifts, you can use your passion to give back.

I have to say the blessings and favor that I receive back is 100+ times the effort that I have put in. There have been times that I have stopped to help someone with their business idea and in return blessings upon blessings are returned back to me in various ways.

Examples:
- I receive favor when I ask others for help, they go above and beyond what I need.
- I have walked in and had dinner in a restaurant, and the manager comes over and says, "Your dinner is free." Even though I have never met them before.
- I have had to make a big purchase, and the salesperson finds an additional discount or gives me something for free.
- I would be in need of some expertise, and I get on the plane and an influential person from that company is sitting in the seat next to me.
- I needed someone to fix something at my house and when the bill comes, they tell me it is now covered under warranty.

- A task that is very big, presents itself as easy and takes less time.

These things happen ALL the time because I continually give back to the world and it comes back in ways small and sometimes very very big!

One relevant verse in the Bible is Proverbs 12:2, which states, "A good man obtains favor from the LORD, but a man of wicked devices he condemns." This highlights the idea that living righteously and with integrity can lead to receiving God's favor.

I wake everyday being humble and thankful. You must keep that energy everyday and all day. I used this example, I'm like a star that keeps on shining brightly and the universe will smile and shine even more brightly back onto me.

Most of us have heard of the idea of Karma. It is a Hindu concept from the Rig Veda (the oldest Hindu holy book). The term Karma has been adopted into Western popular culture, often used to describe the idea that "what goes around, comes around."

So what you put out is what is coming back to you. I firmly believe in this concept, so that is why I say it's important to shine your bright light.

Karma refers to the principle of cause and effect, where a person's actions (good or bad) influence their future experiences.

I want to share with you some modern Western thoughts about Karma:

- **Cause and Effect**

Karma suggests that every action has consequences. Good actions lead to positive outcomes, while bad actions lead to negative outcomes.

- **Moral Responsibility**

It emphasizes moral responsibility, encouraging individuals to act ethically and with good intentions.

- **Rebirth and Samsara**

In many traditions, karma is linked to the cycle of rebirth (samsara). The quality of one's actions in this life can affect their future lives.

Karma is often misunderstood as fate or destiny. However, it is more about the natural consequences of one's actions rather than a predetermined fate.

Look back at this past month, have you found ways to give back? That does not mean to spend time with people, places, or things that don't benefit from your expertise, money or time. I don't want you to go out and run around trying to fix everything that you see. That may get you off focus on your priorities. But as you progress can you stop once and a while and help others in so many ways! You can do it!

CHAPTER 13 EXERCISES

The goal of this exercise is to help you think about whether you have been giving back and create a small list of things that you can do going forward.

List different ways you give back? If you don't give back, why do you think that is?

List different ways that you have not previously thought about, on how to use your expertise to give back. Put those examples in the areas listed below.

List different ways that you have not previously thought about, on how to use your expertise to give back. Put those examples in the areas listed below.

Volunteer your time

Donate

Support a local business

Mentor or tutor

Organize a community event

Pay it forward

Use your skills

Advocate for a cause

Care for the elderly or infirm

Environmental efforts

List all of the gifts you have that you can use to help others below. Choose one that brings you joy and write out 10 ways you could use that gift in the next month.

ABOUT THE AUTHOR

LaSonjia "LJ" Jack is a powerhouse businesswoman who has made her mark on the world. In 2023, LJ made history by becoming the first African American majority owner of an East Coast Hockey League (ECHL) team, the Allen Americans, which is a venture she shares with her son, former linebacker for the NFL Jacksonville Jaguars and The Pittsburgh Steelers, Myles Jack. LJ's expertise in organizational management and ability to propel a business forward have earned her executive-level positions at some of the country's tops firms, such as Microsoft, AT&T, T-Mobile, and Cox.

LJ proudly wears many hats, including Sports Mom, Sports Team Owner, Mommy Manager, Business Coach and Mentor, Board Member, and CEO of the Jack Family businesses. LJ is the proud mother of two accomplished sons, Myles and Jahlen.

Despite her humble beginnings, including bouncing back after divorce, LJ managed to carve her own path to success. She holds a Bachelor of Science in business management and a Master of Science in organizational management. The LJ Way - The Roadmap To Your Journey From Poverty to Plenty is LJ's literary debut.

www.ingramcontent.com/pod-product-compliance
Lightning Source LLC
Chambersburg PA
CBHW050857160426
43194CB00011B/2189